Author & photographer: Thierry Hebbelinck

© 2020 Thierry Hebbelinck

Self-publishing: "Galerie Hotel Saint-Michel".

All rights reserved:

This book or any portion thereof
may not be reproduced or used in any manner whatsoever
without the express written permission of the author may be reproduced,
distributed, or transmitted in any form or by any means, including
photocopying, recording, or other electronic or mechanical methods,
without the prior written permission.

Thierry Hebbelinck is a member of Sabam:

Sabam is a Belgian association of authors
composers and publishers.

Photo book southwest coast Tenerife.(Landscape format).

The Canaries are one of the most interesting tourist destinations for Northern & Western Europeans in wintertime. Always springtime. Especially the south of Gran Canaria & Tenerife.
This coffee heavy image book shows photos of the touristic southwest beach district of Tenerife: Arona, Santa Cruz de Tenerife, island of Spain.

Photos taken during a walk of 2,1km (1,3miles) from Playa de Las Américas to Playa Los Cristianos.
Photo shoot beaches:
Playa Las Américas, Playa Del Camison, Playa Las Vistas, Playa Los Cristianos and Montaña Chayofita.
- Costa La Caleta de Adeje, Santa Cruz de Tenerife, Spain 8,4km (5 miles) from Playa Las Américas.

Panoramic landscapes are made from multiple vertical or horizontal shots with a full frame Dslr camera and a tilt/shift perspective correction prime lens. Afterwards the images were stitched together with software on computer.
All the photos are shot during a walk, like a tourist would leave the hotel to make an afternoon walk.
Adeje photo shoot : taxi transfer from Playa Las Américas to Adeje.

Photographer: Thierry Hebbelinck

Coffee book about Tenerife, a Canary Island best sunny winter destination photographed.

Serie: horizontal panoramic landscapes.

Author & photographer

Thierry Hebbelinck

Self-publishing by
Galerie Hotel Saint-Michel

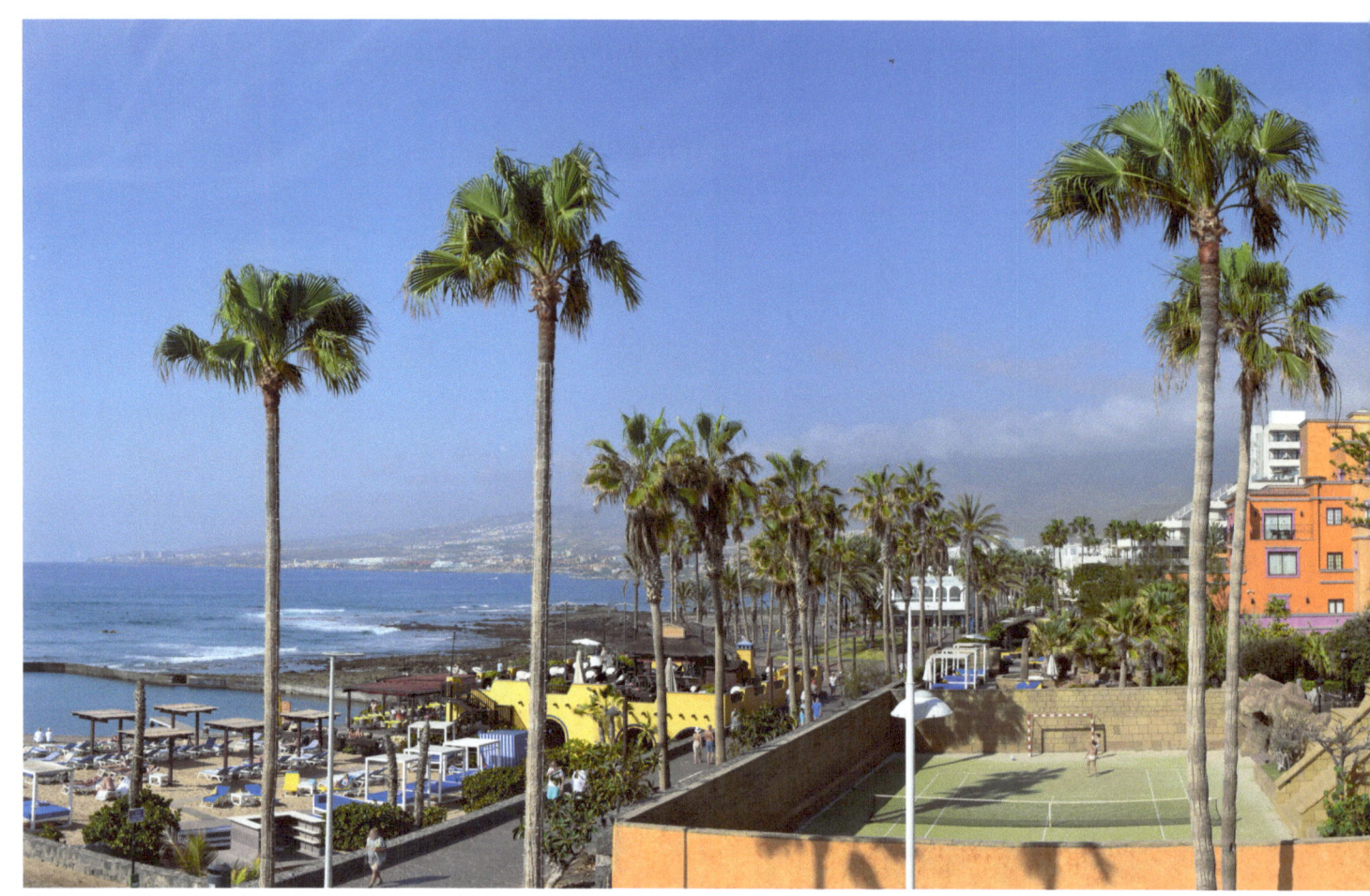

Panoramic sea view from Paseo Orinoco on - Playa las Américas, Arona, Santa Cruz de Tenerife.

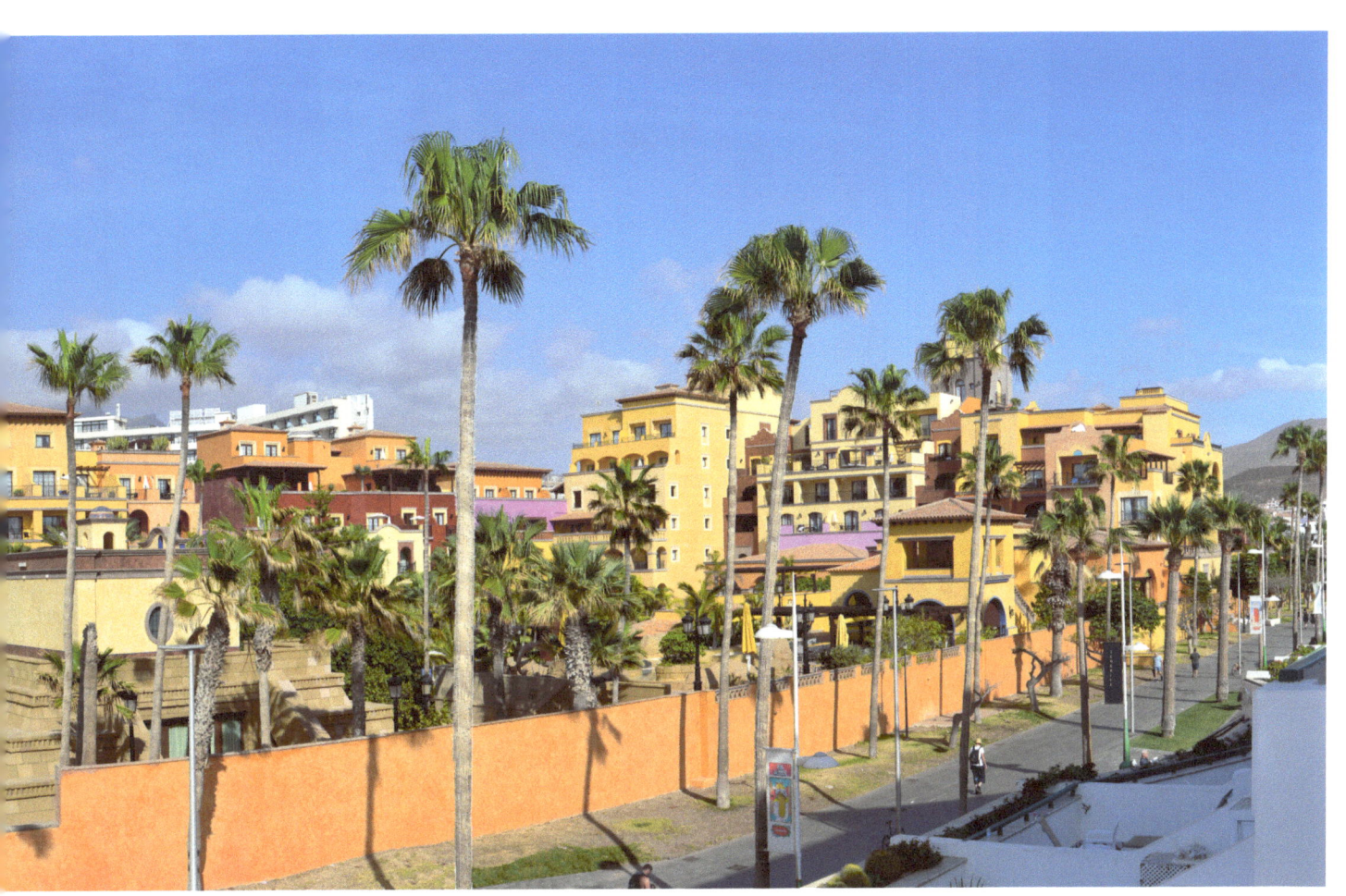

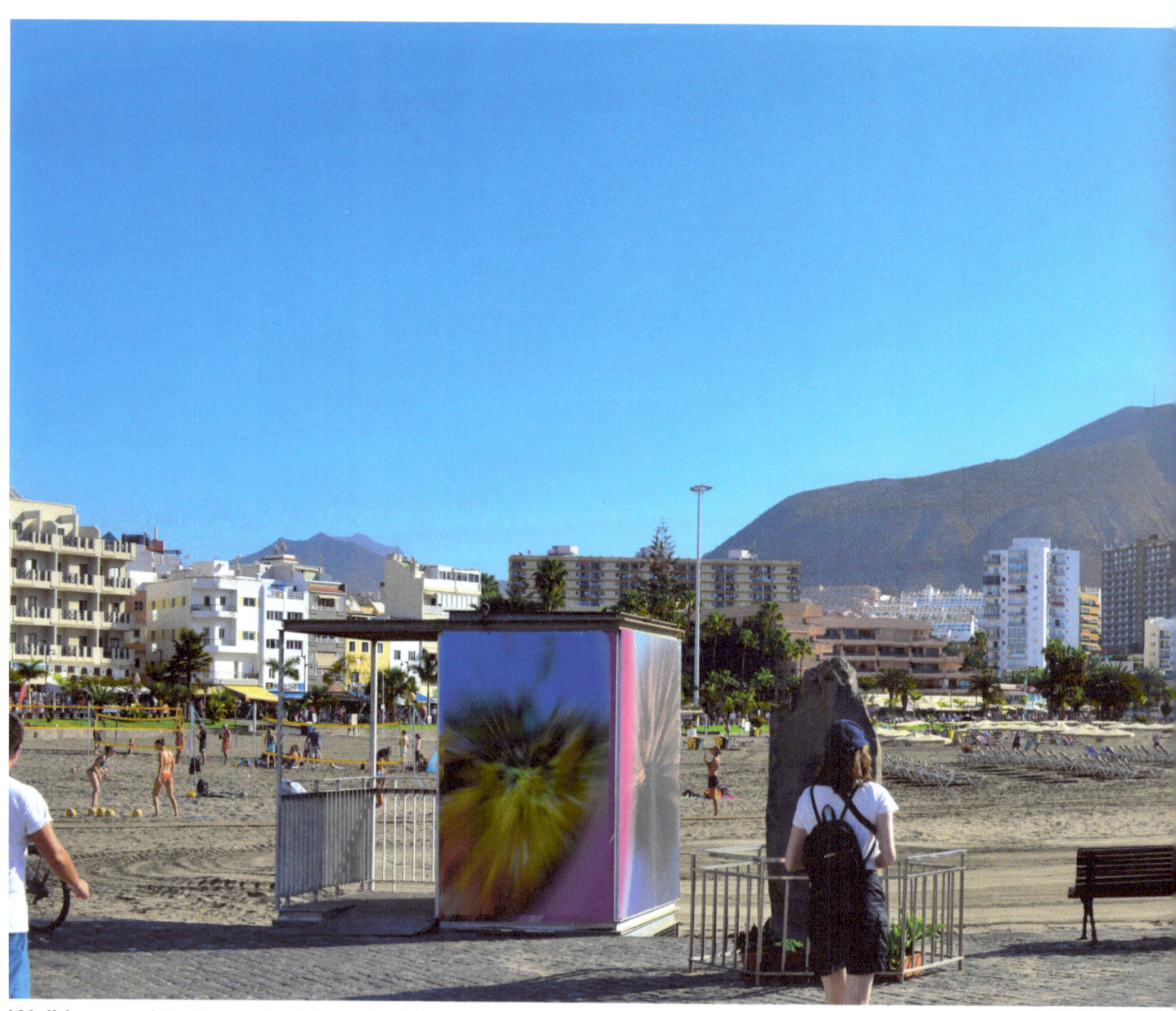
Walking road to the port of Los Cristianos.

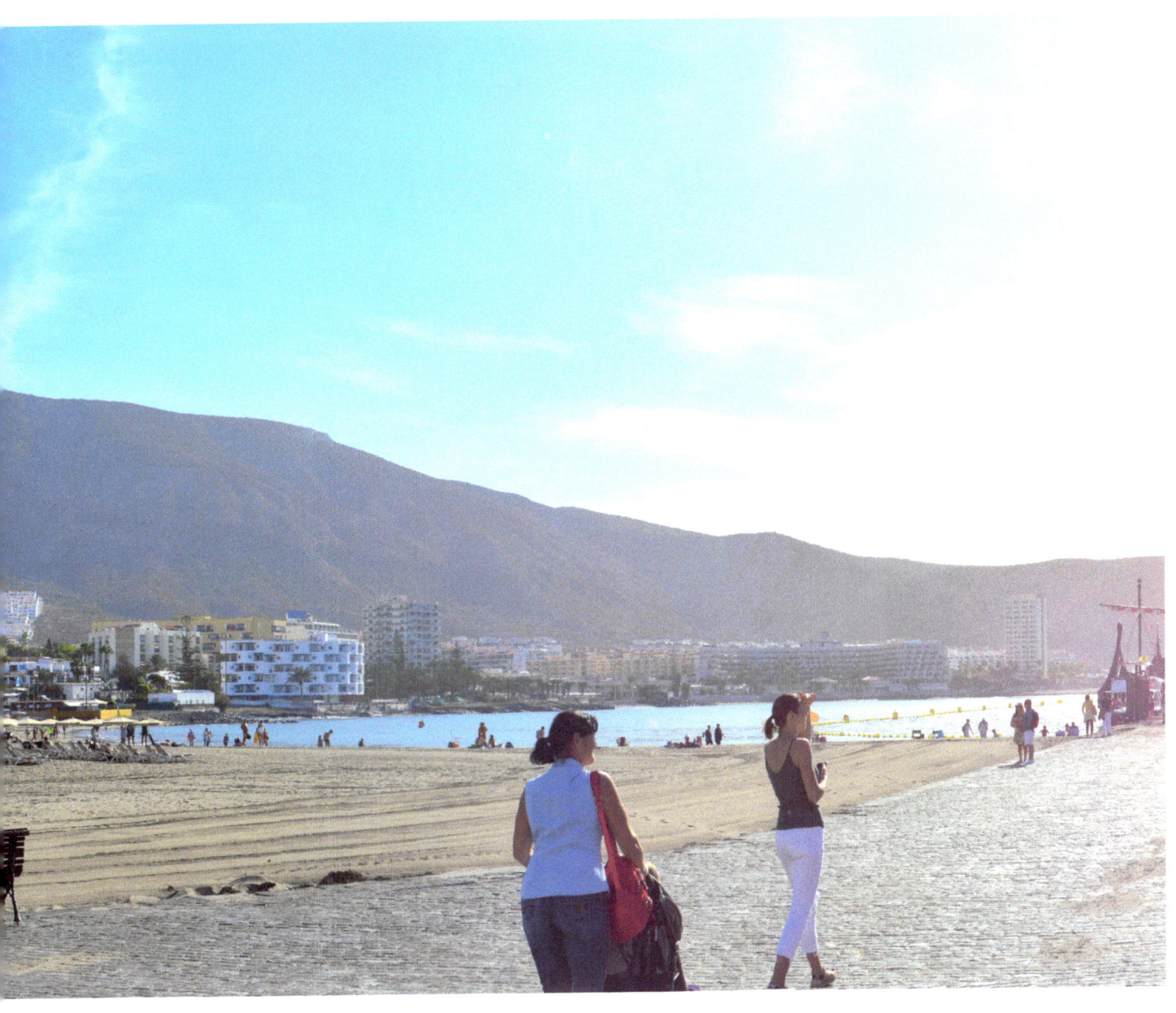

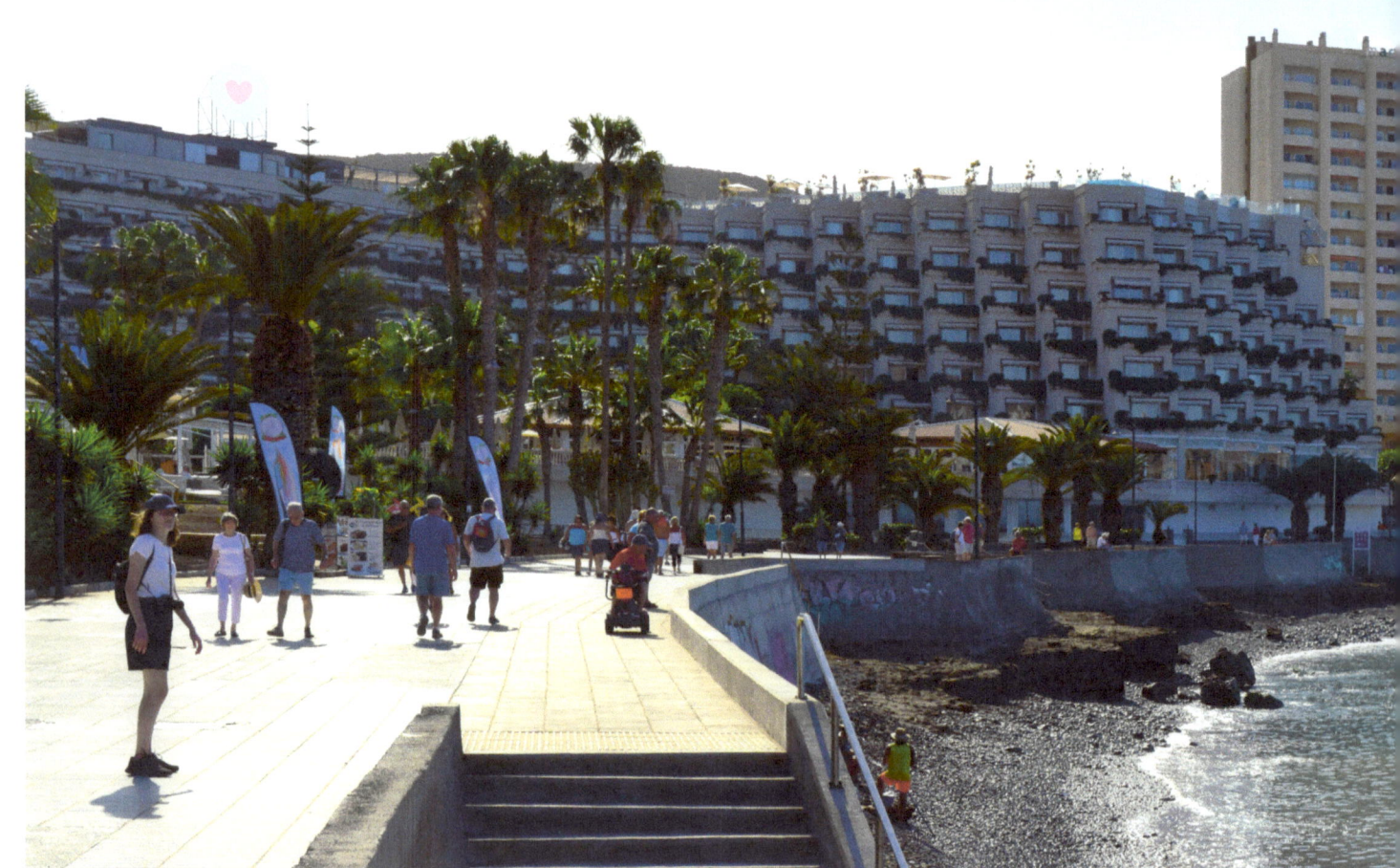

View on Playa de Los Tarajales.

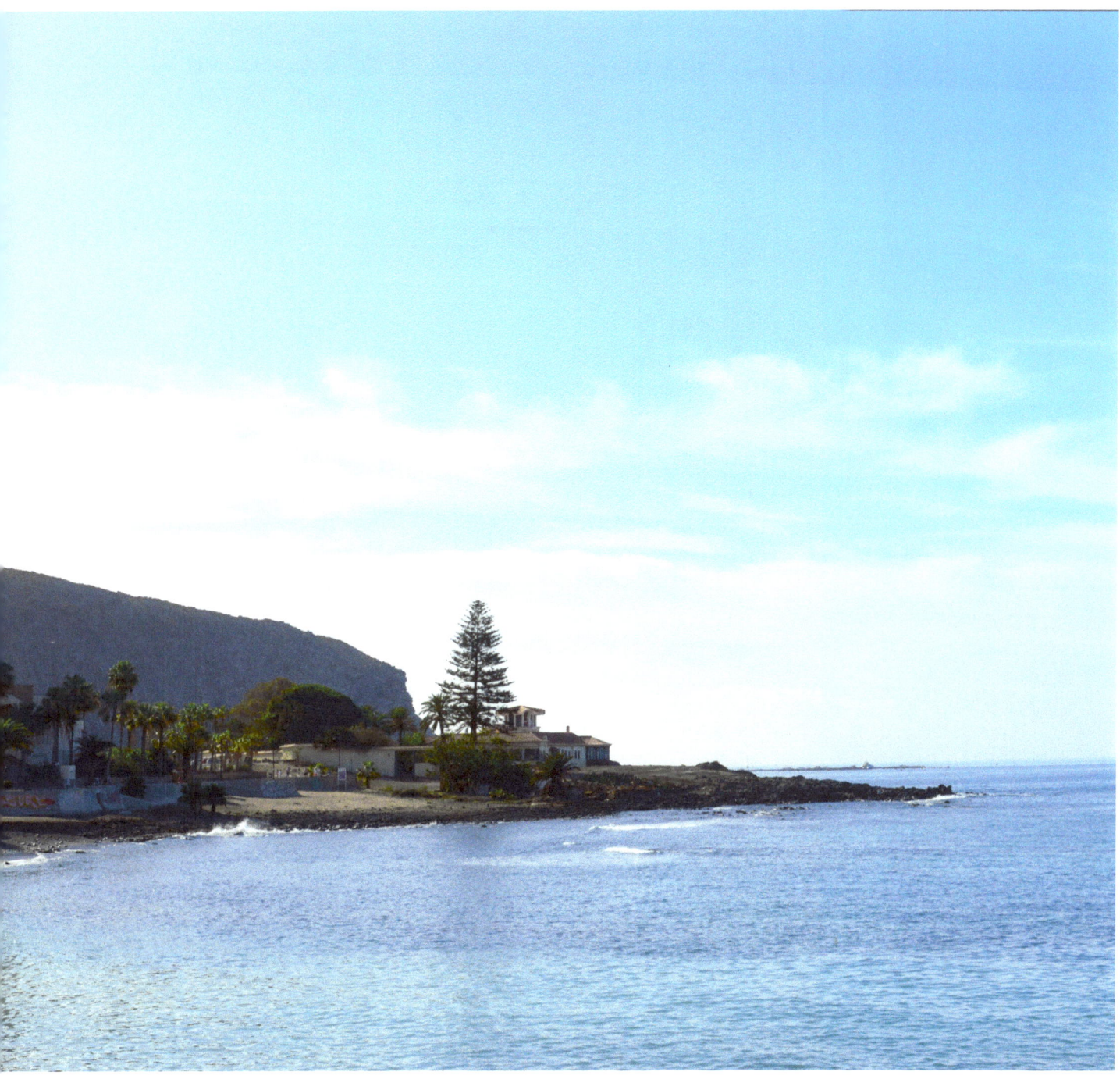

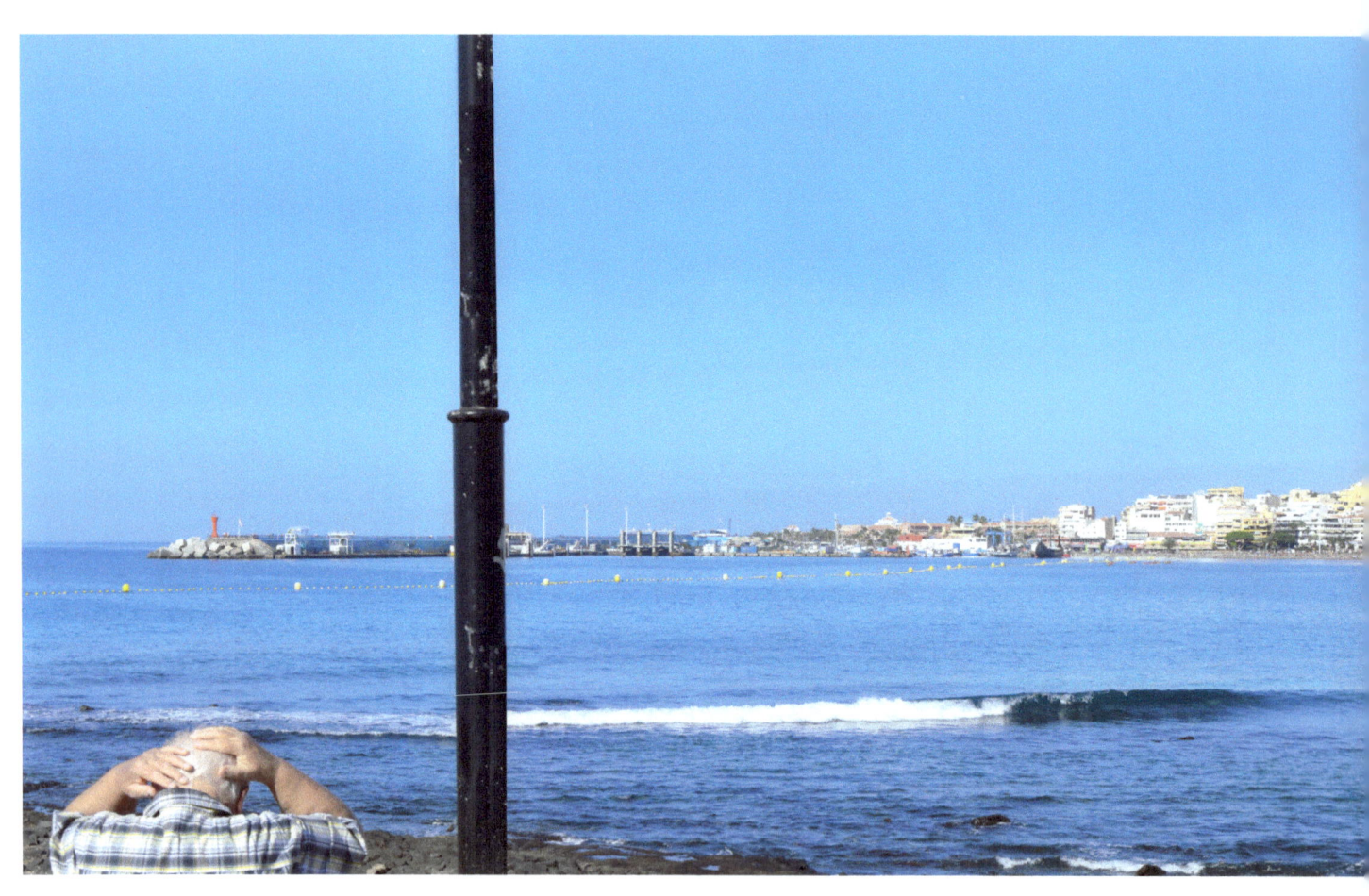

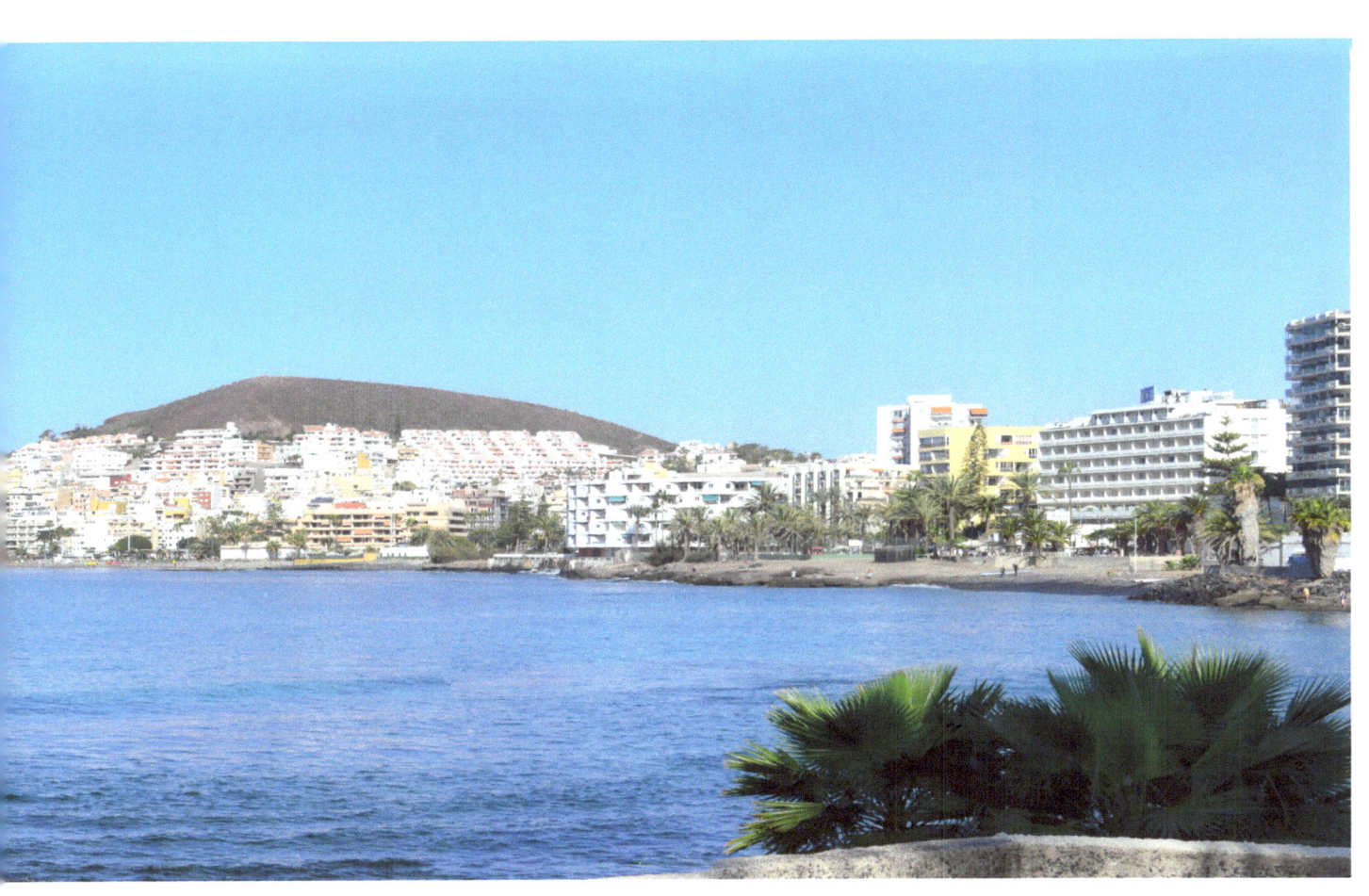

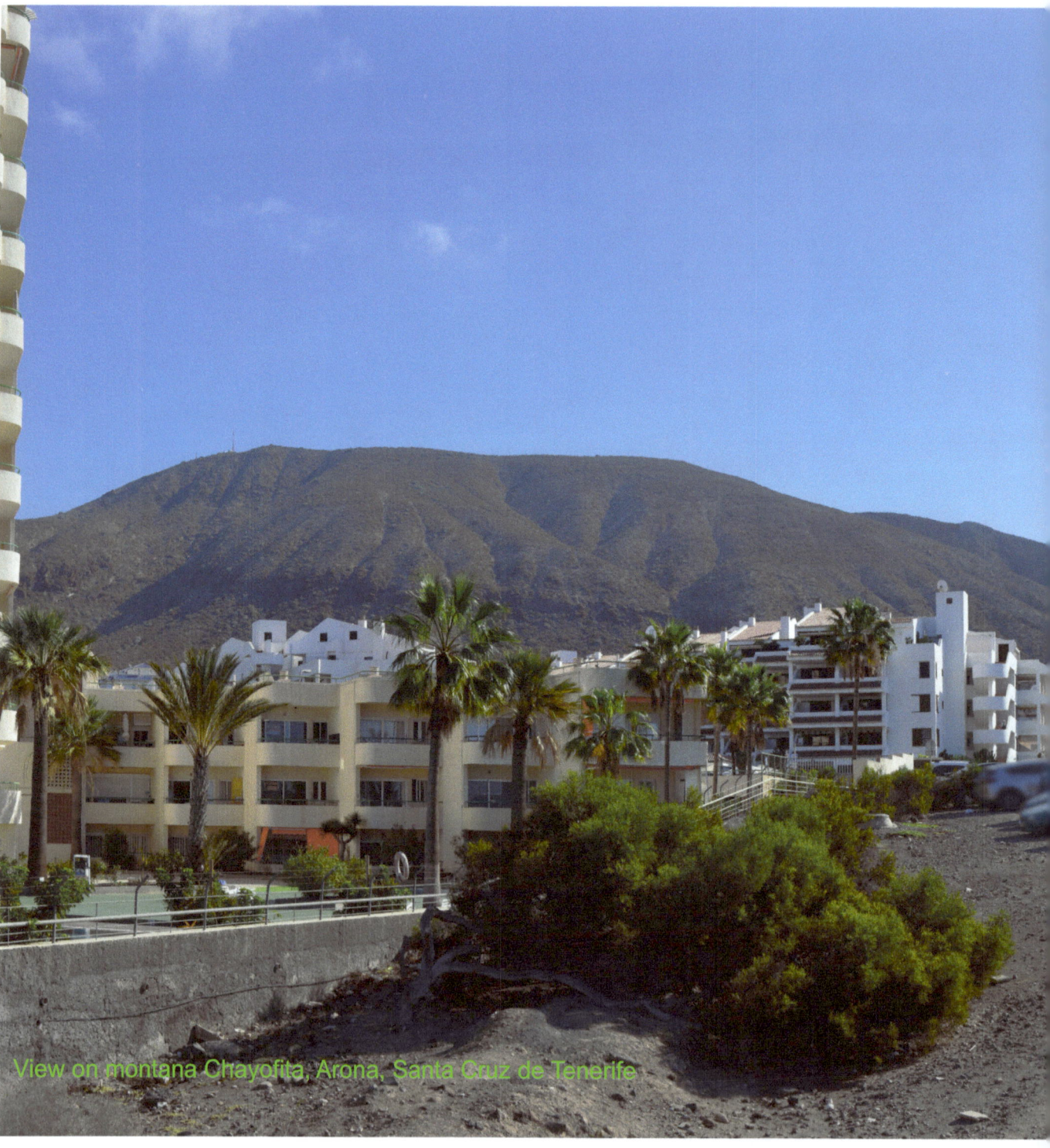

View on montana Chayofita, Arona, Santa Cruz de Tenerife

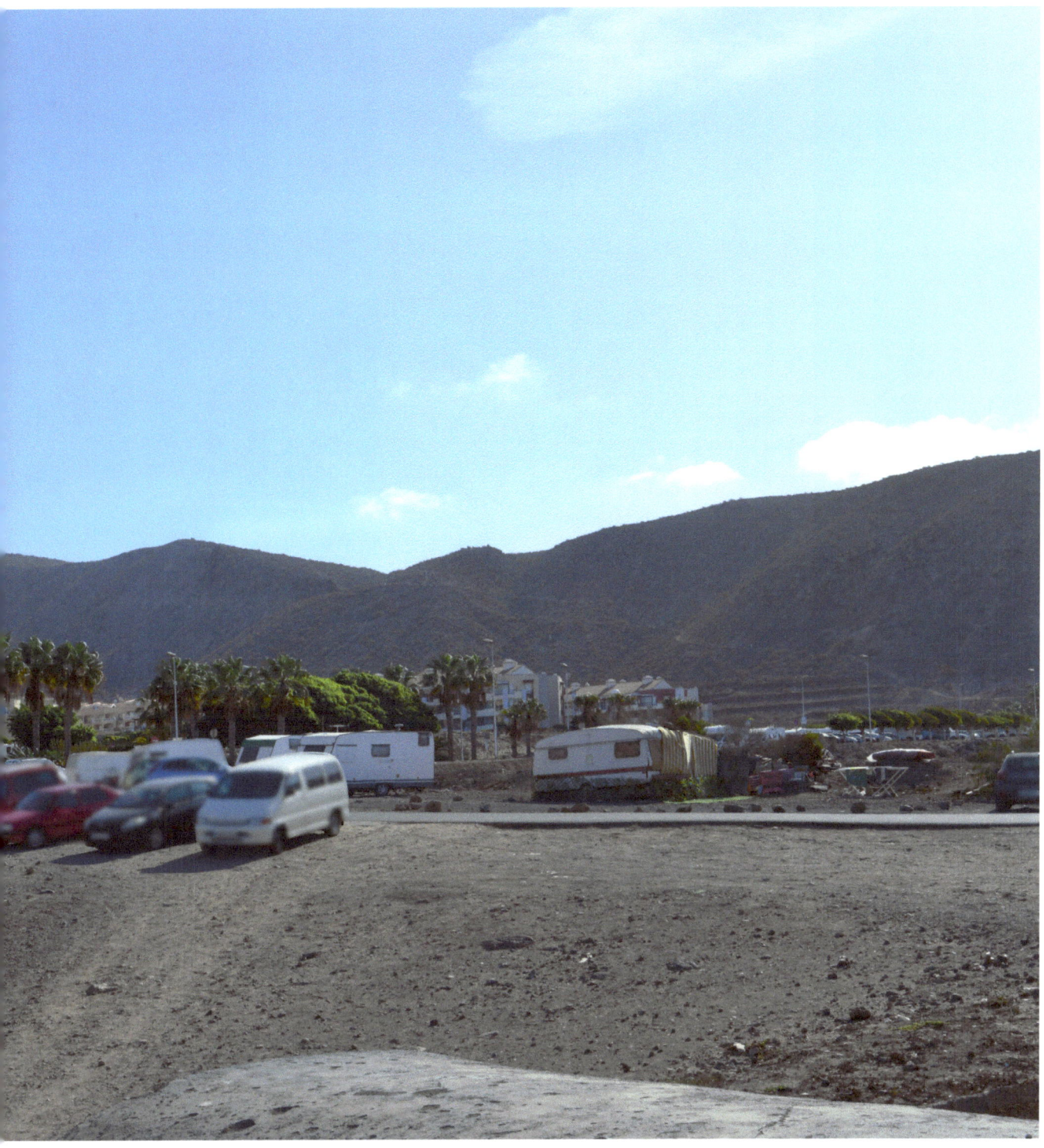

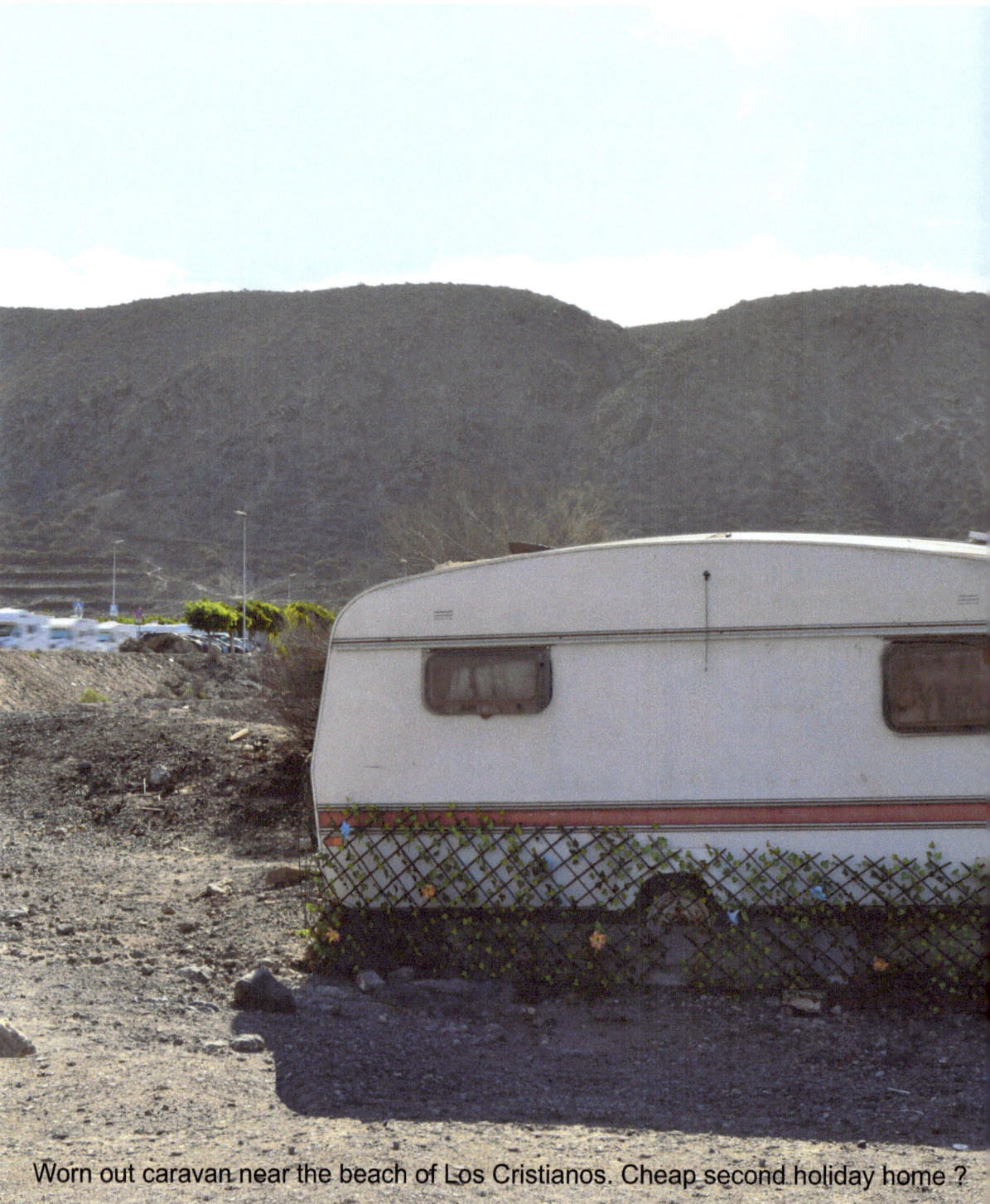

Worn out caravan near the beach of Los Cristianos. Cheap second holiday home ?

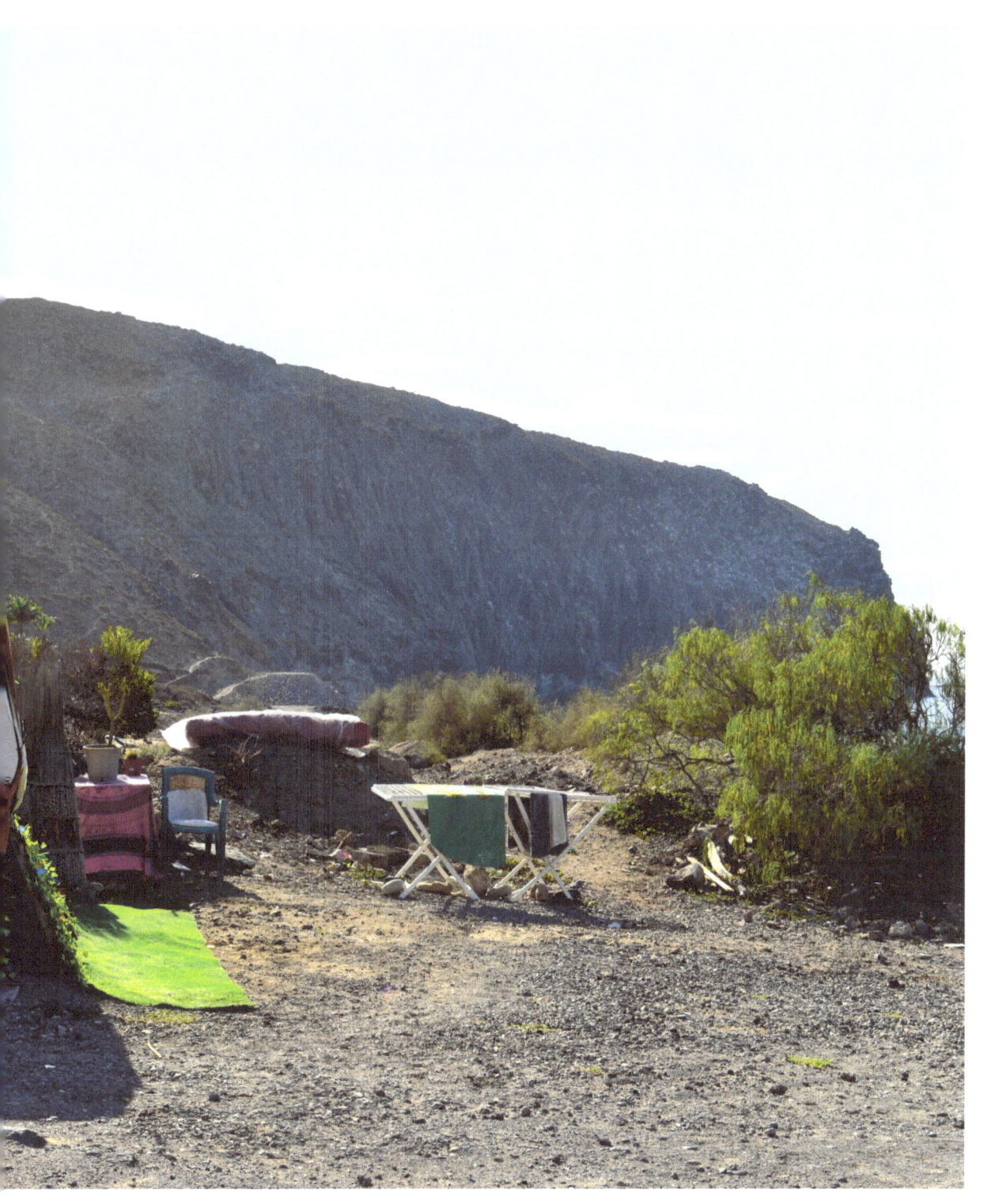

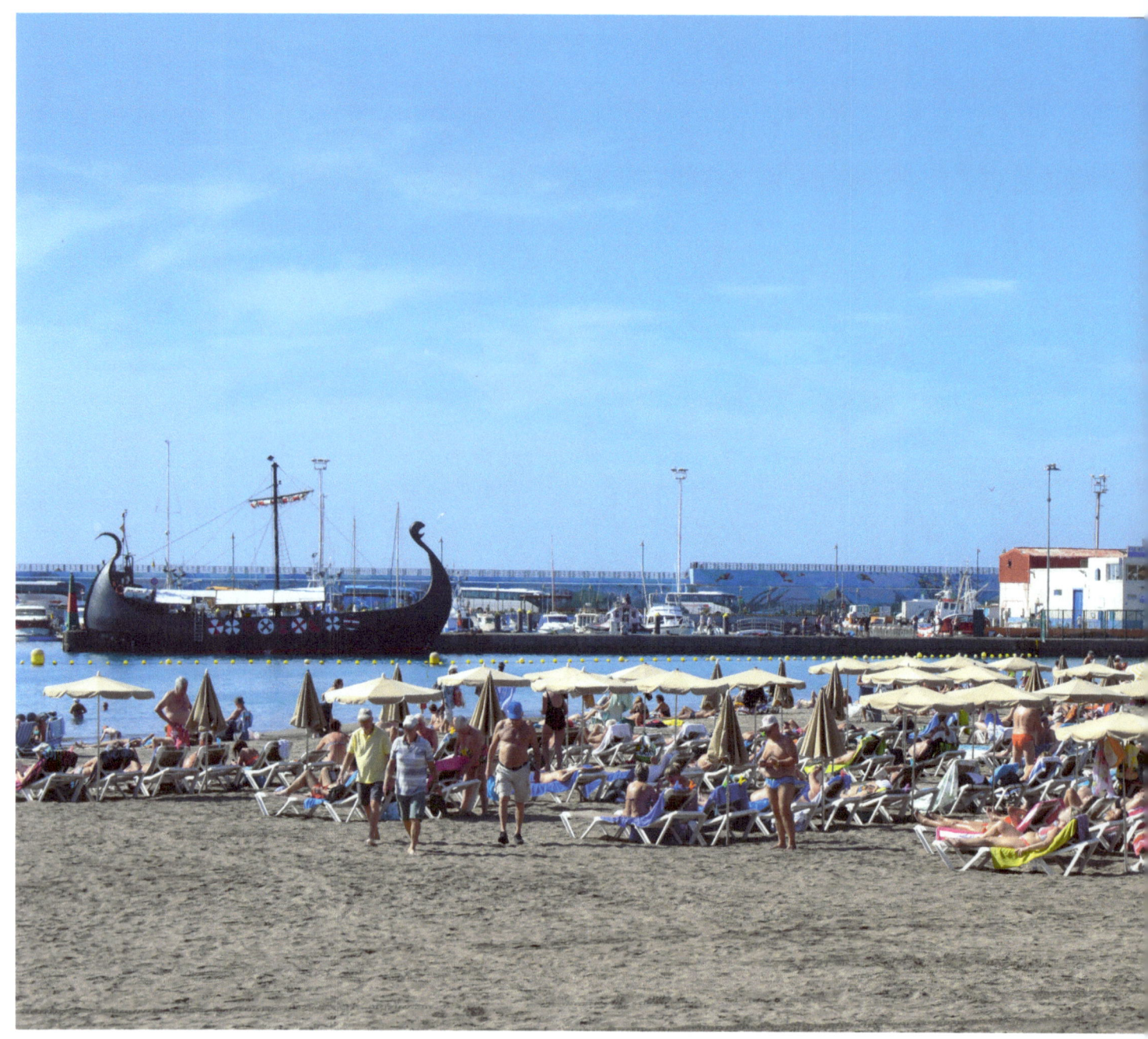

Beach & harbour Los Cristianos

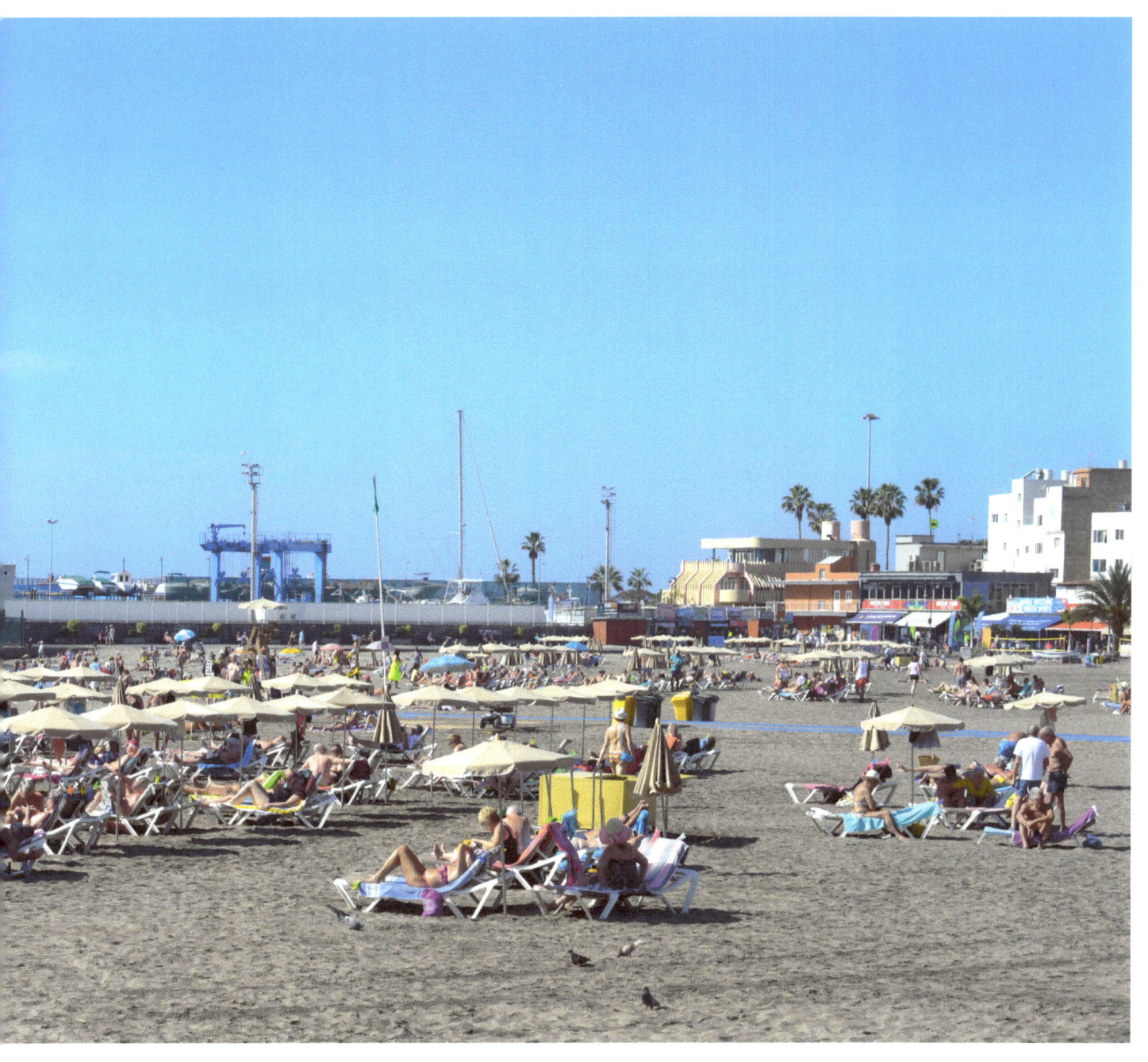

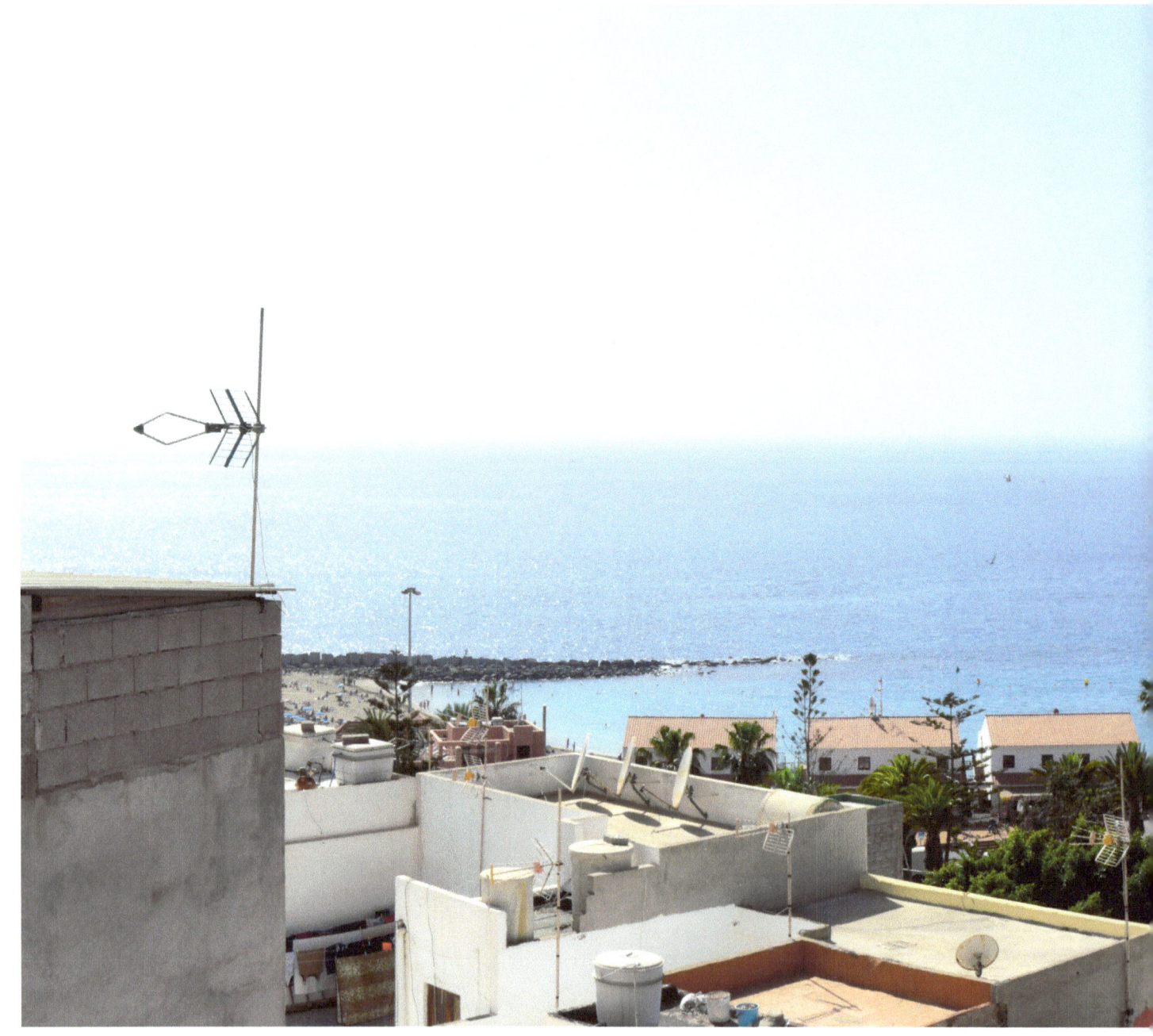

Seascape skyline Los Cristianos.

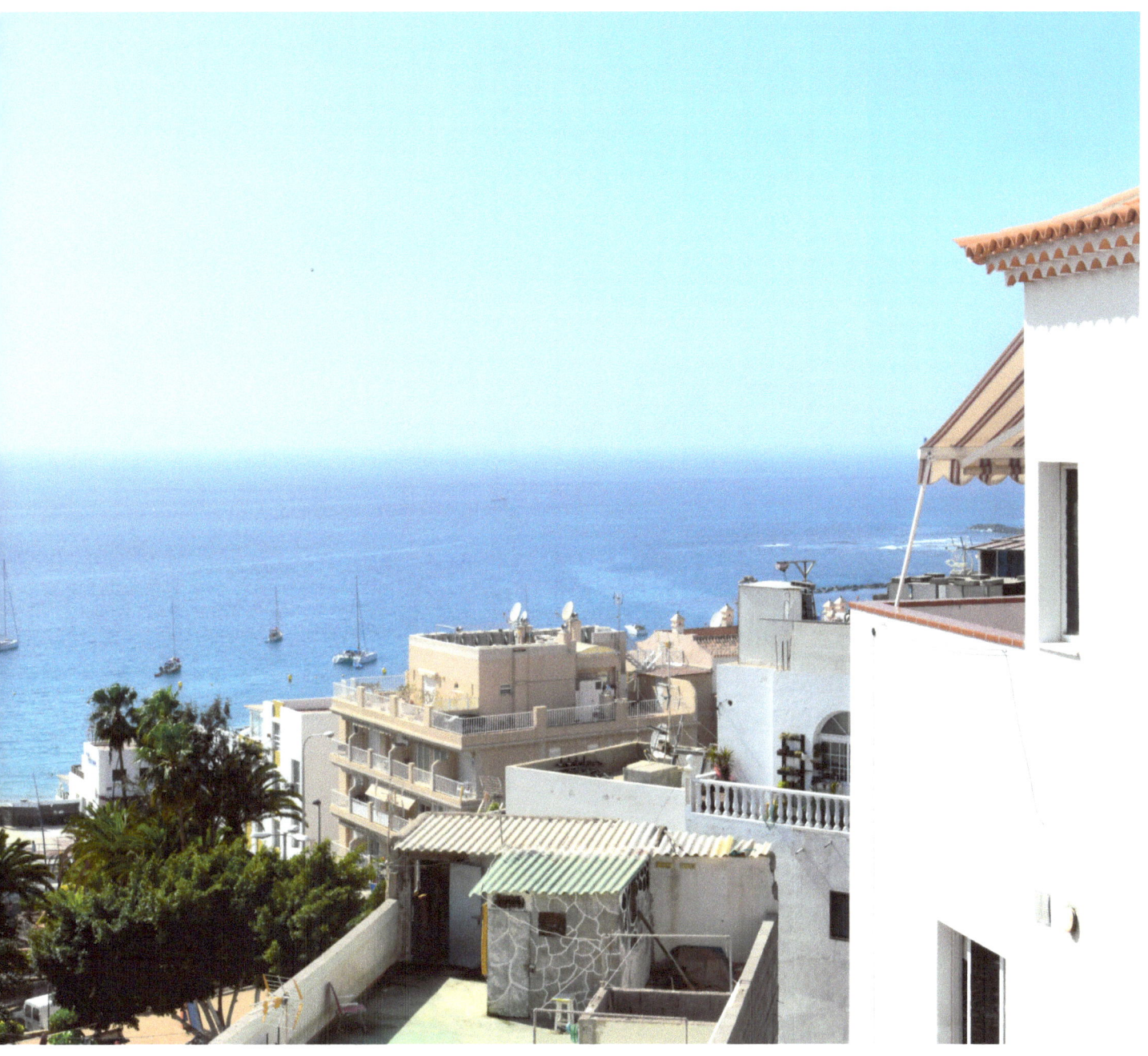

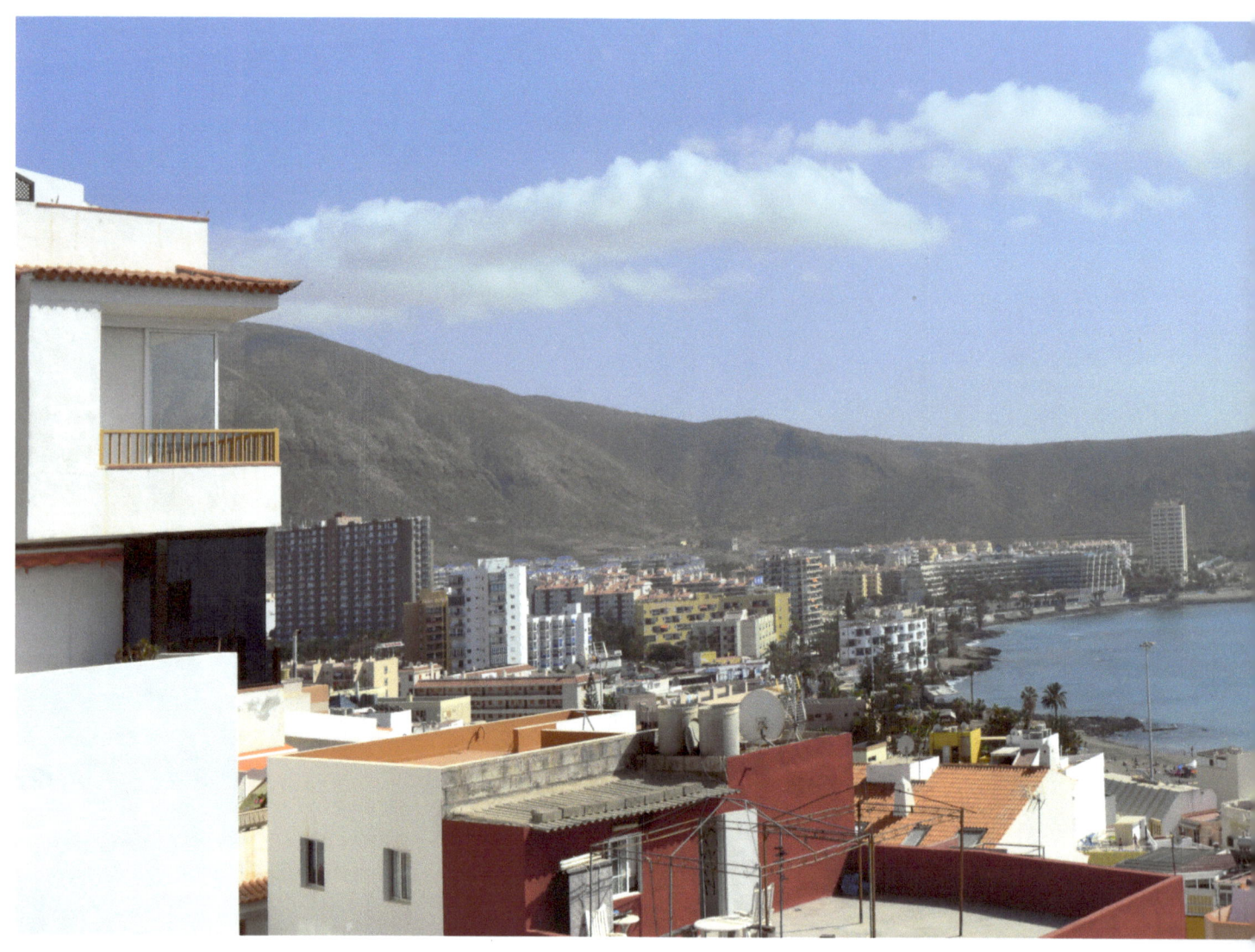
Skyline harbour Los Cristianos

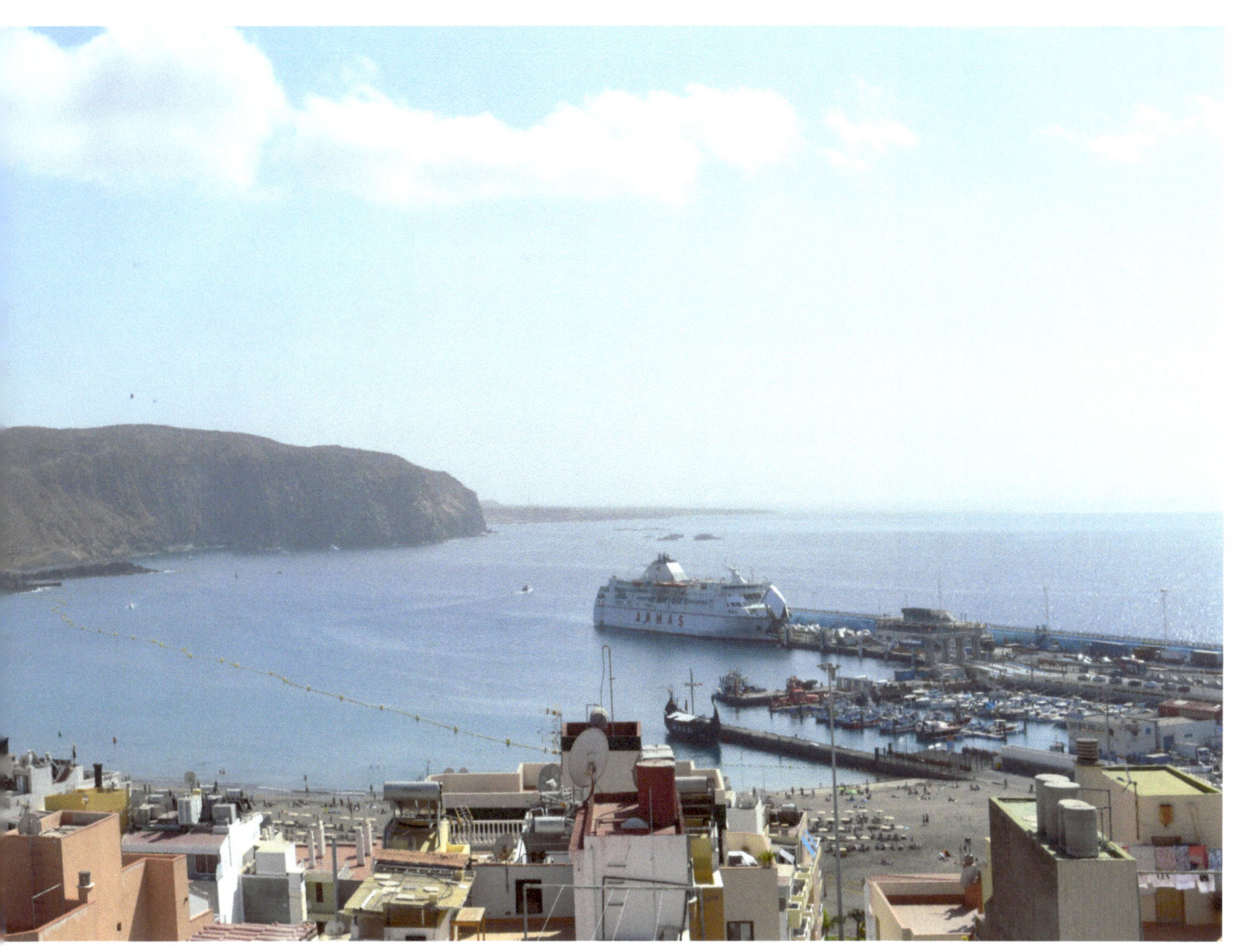

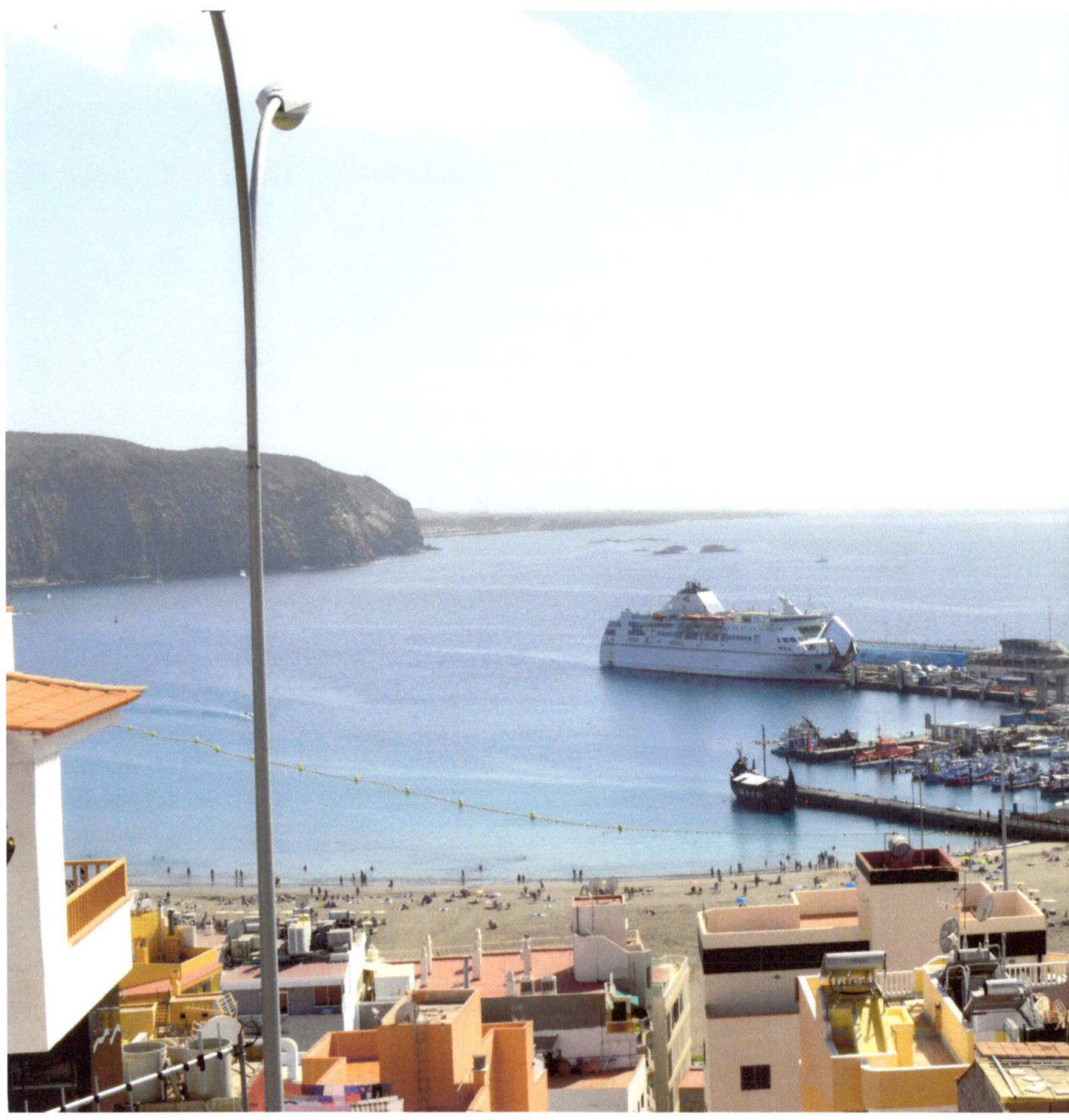

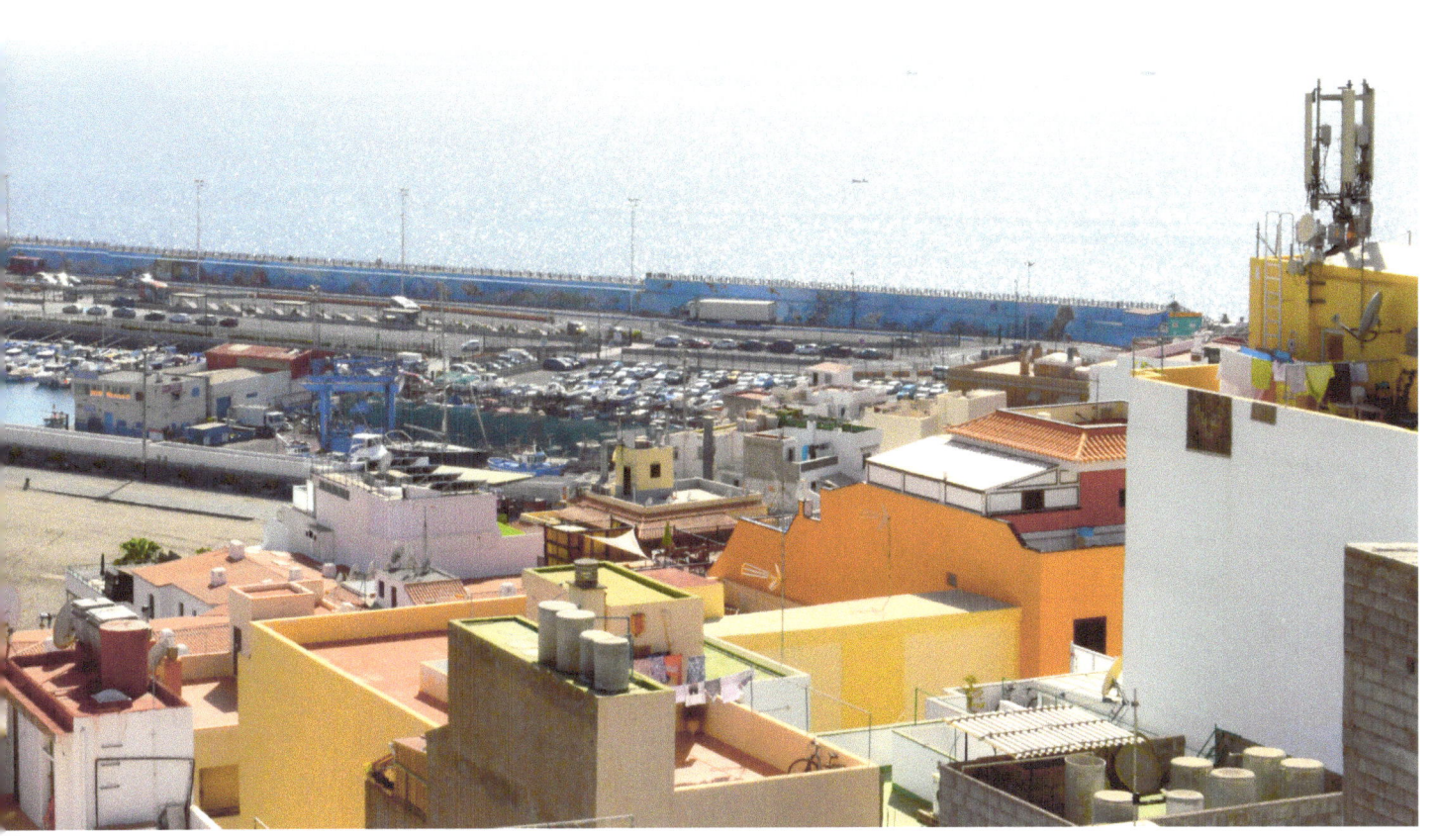

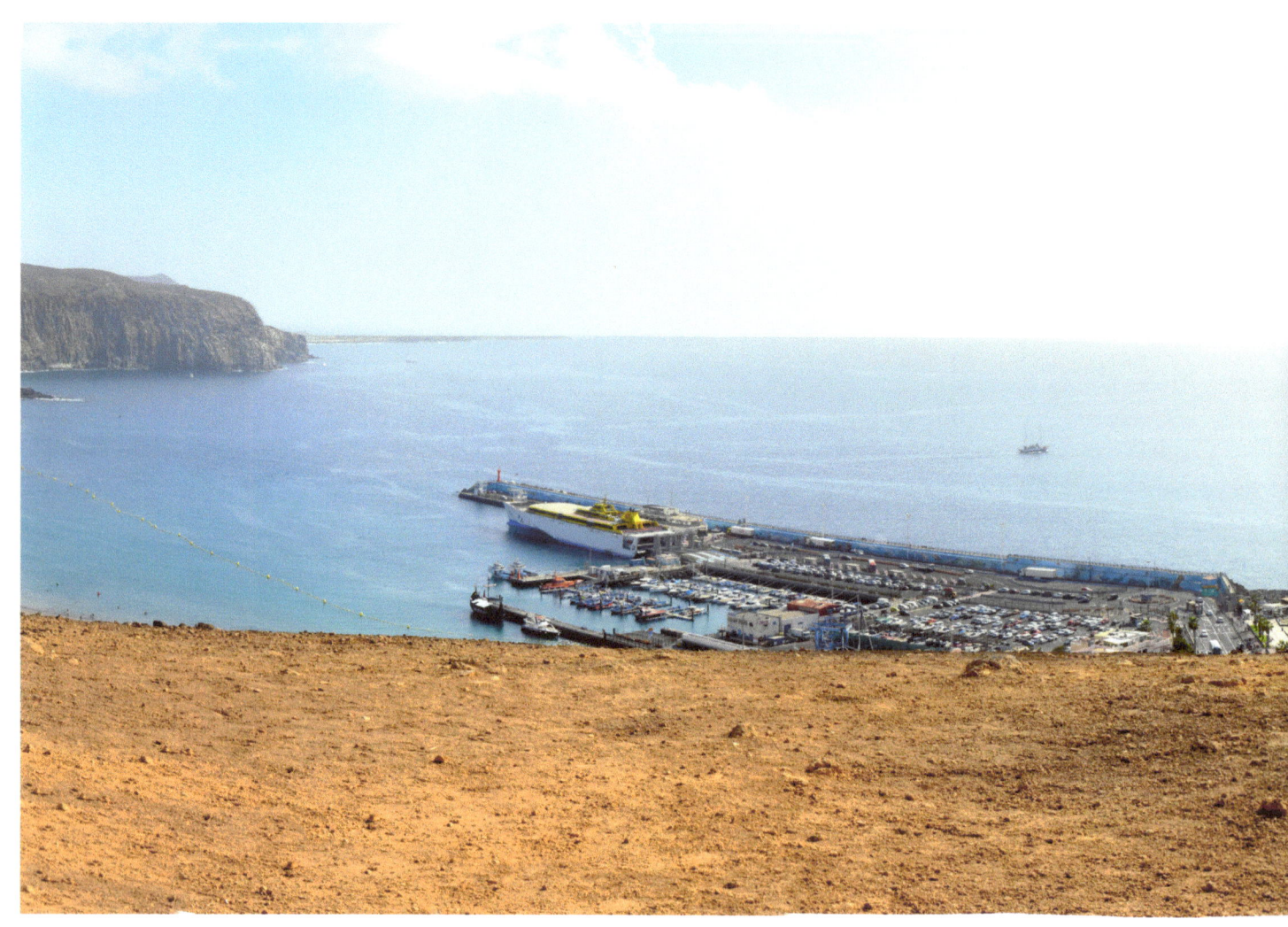
Skyline harbour Los Cristianos, view from montana Chayofita.

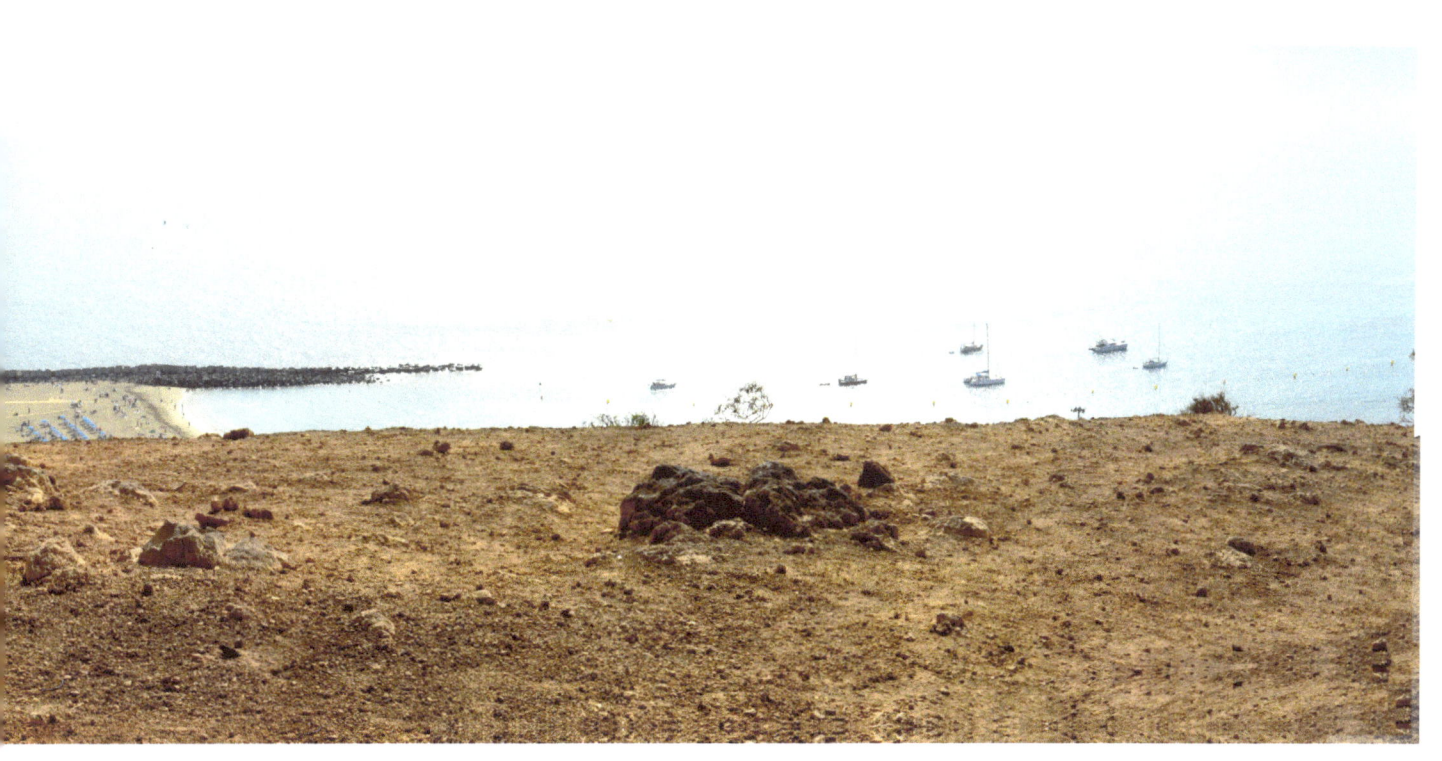

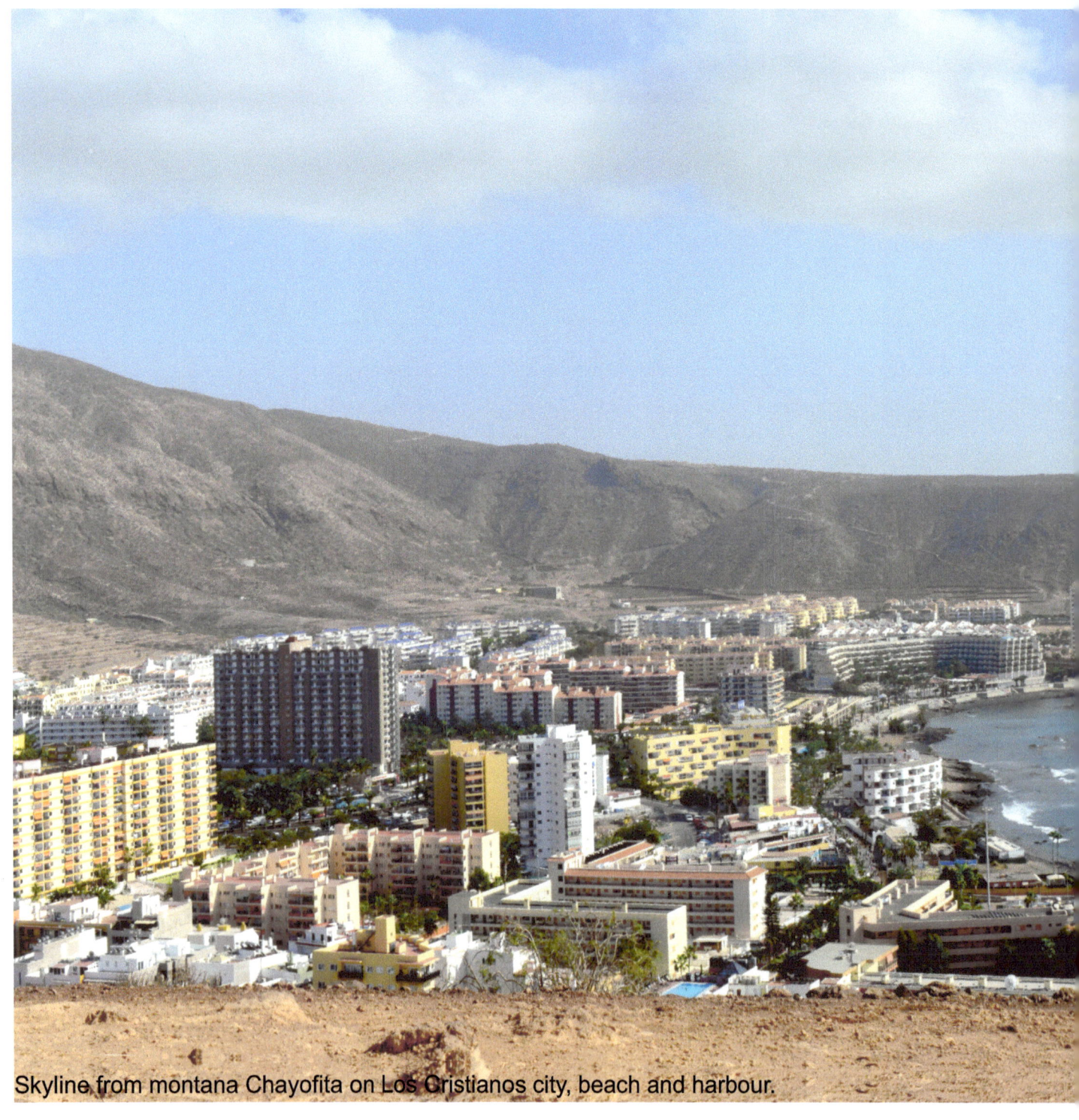
Skyline from montana Chayofita on Los Cristianos city, beach and harbour.

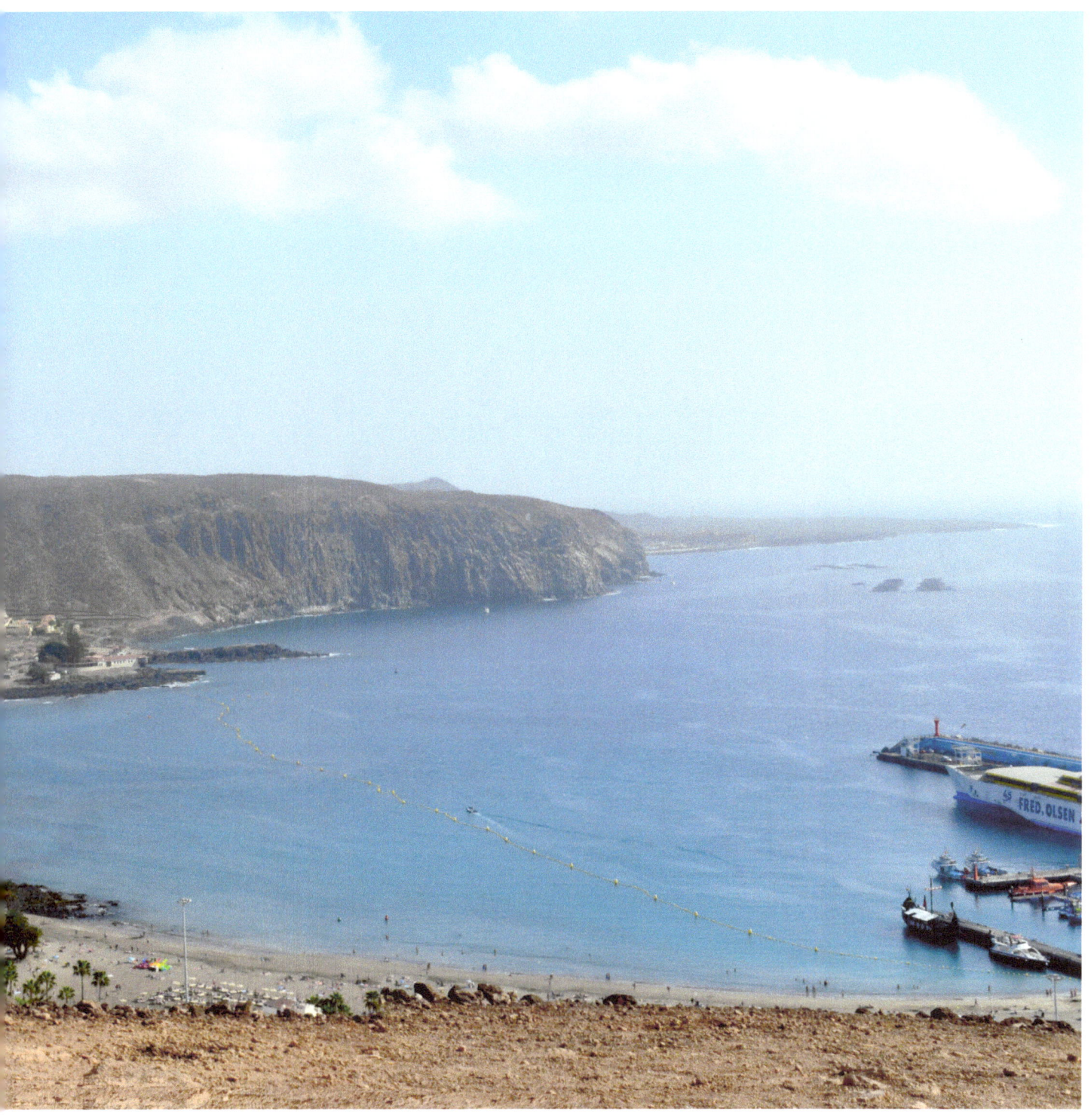

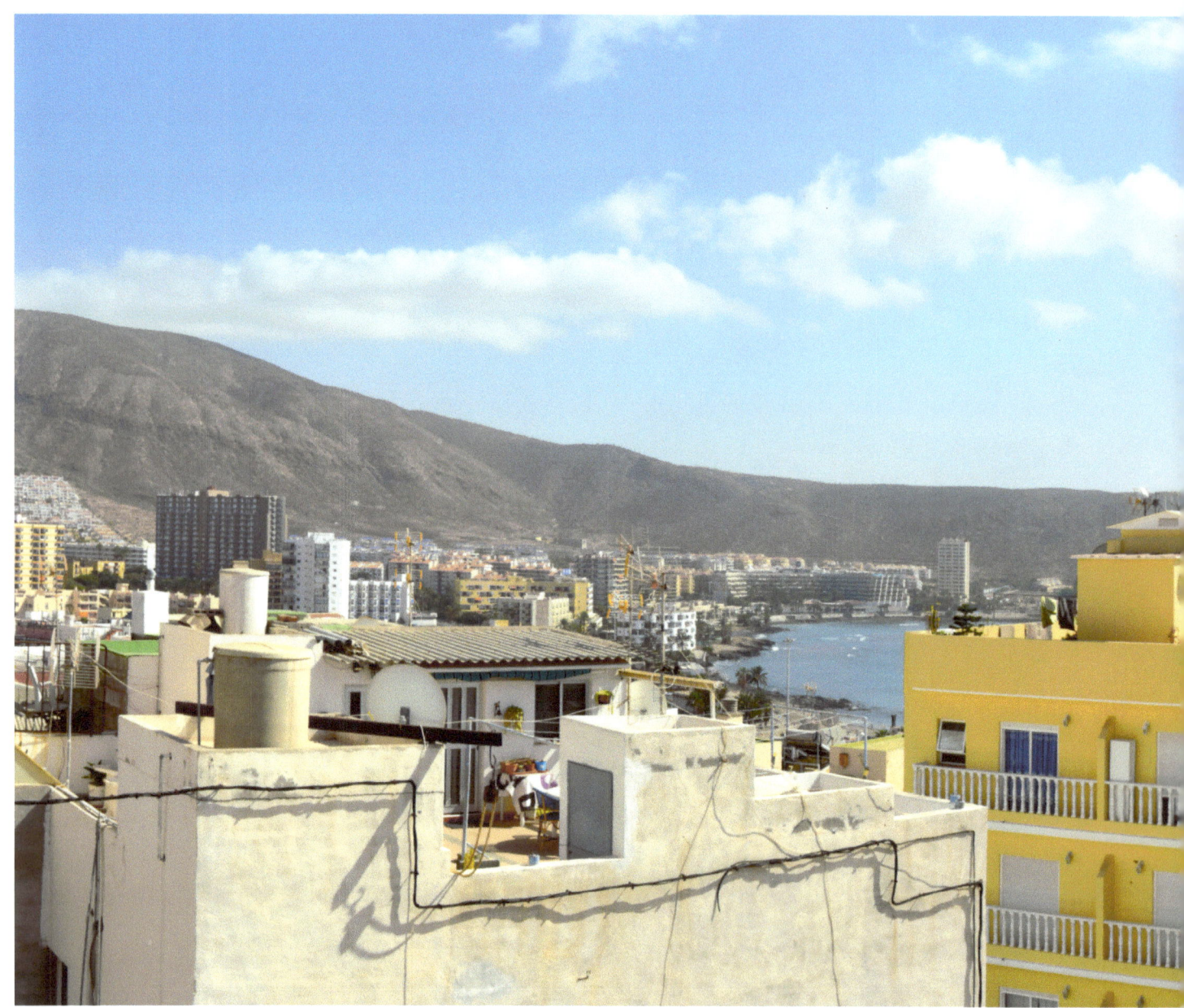

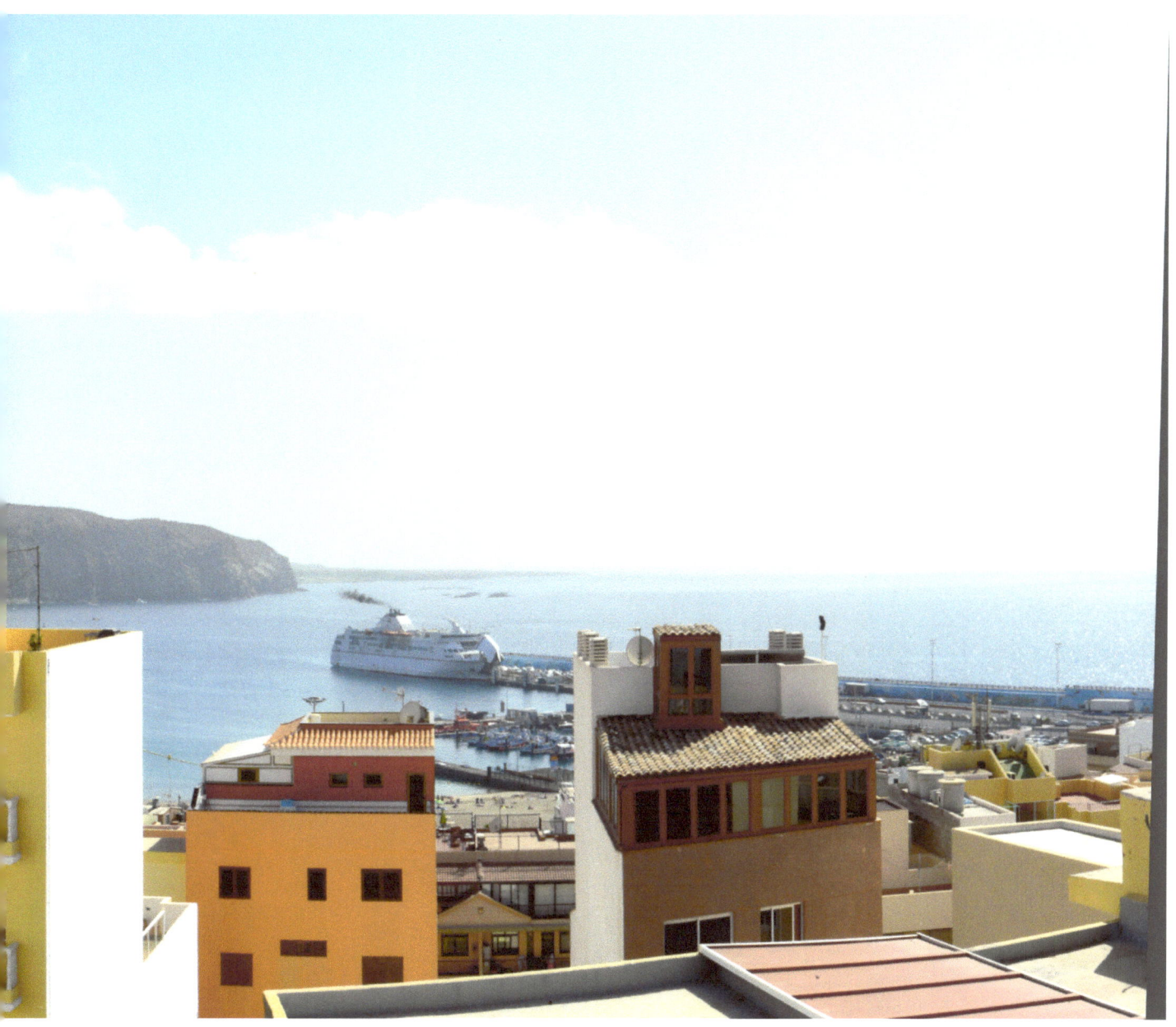

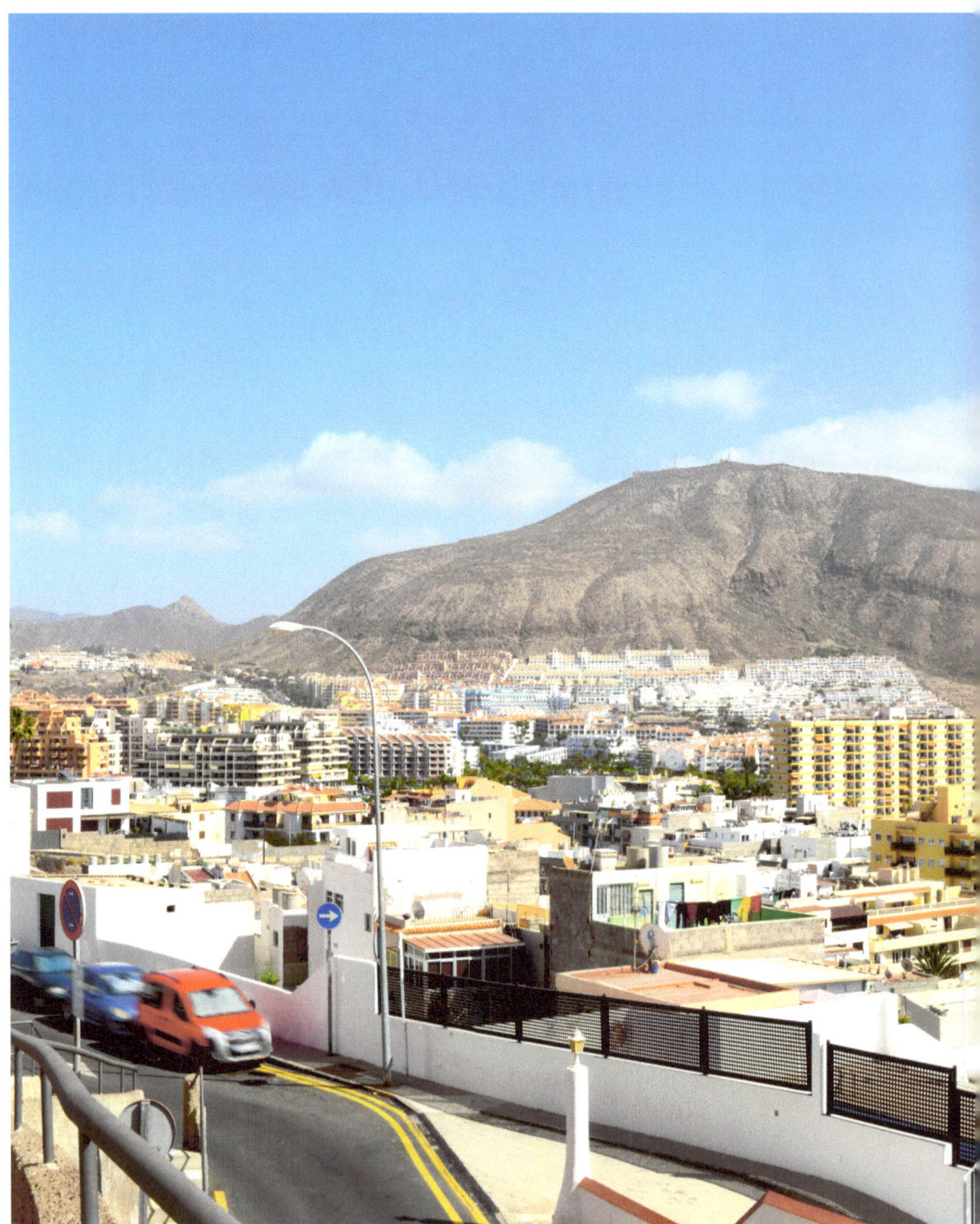

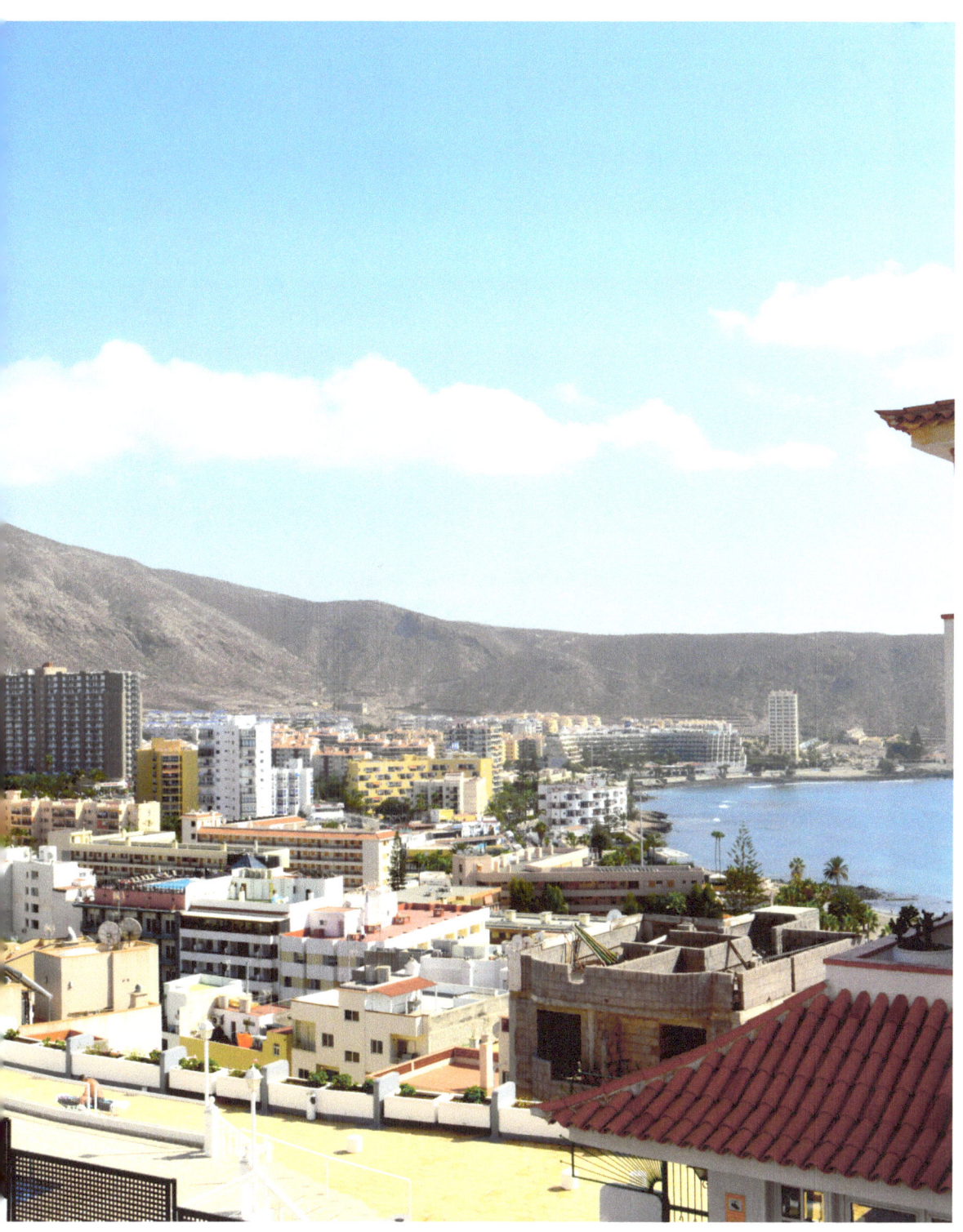

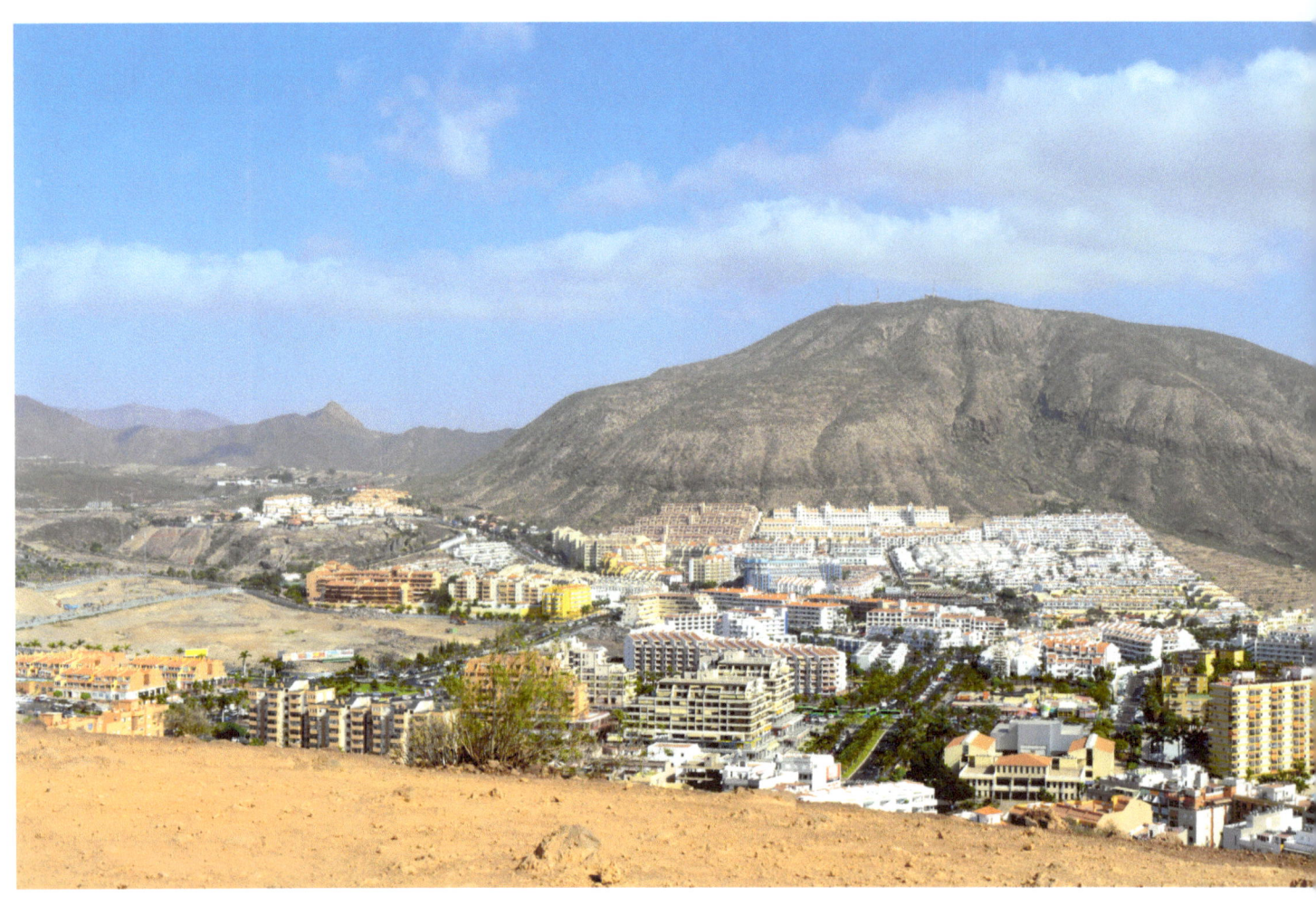

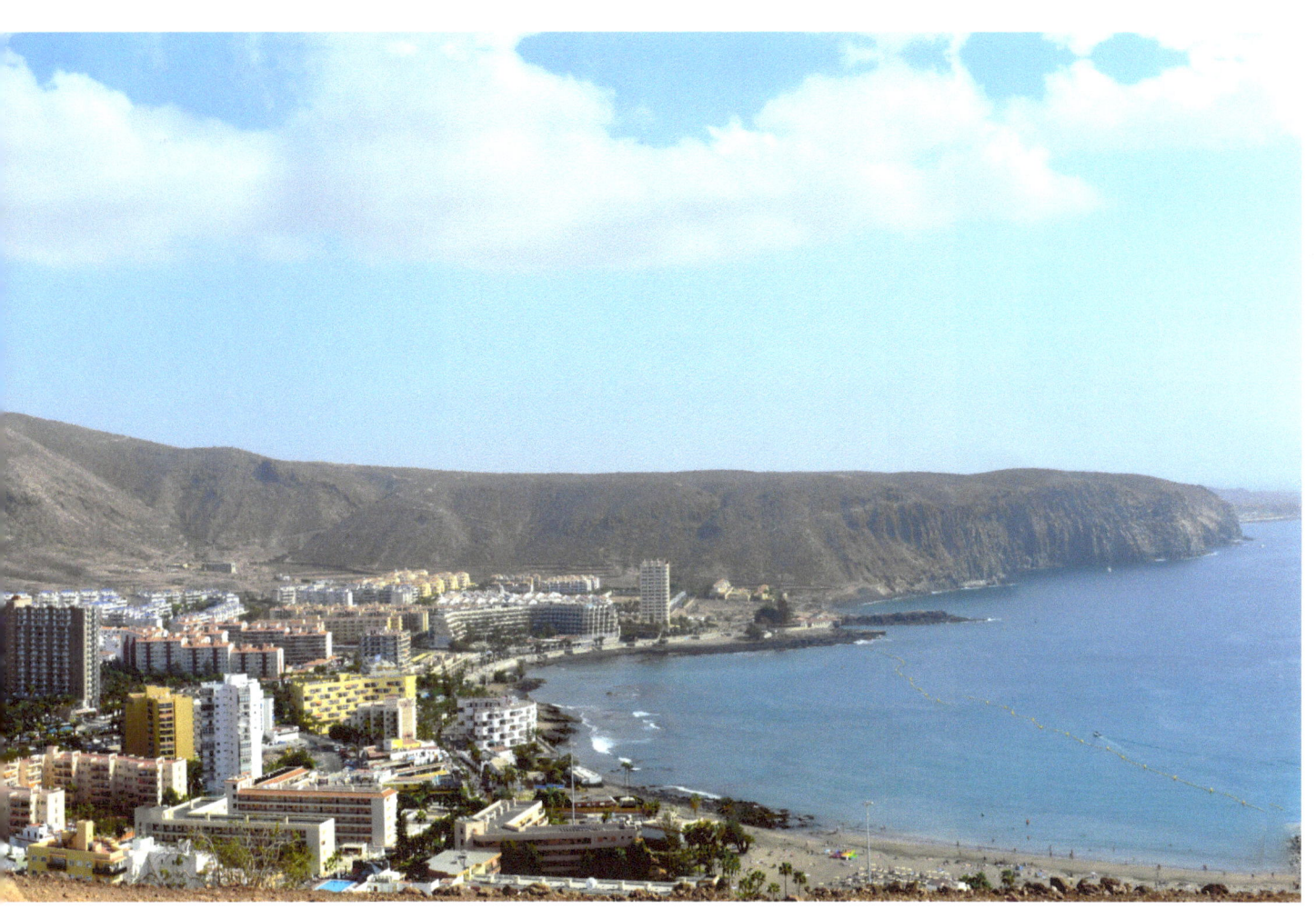

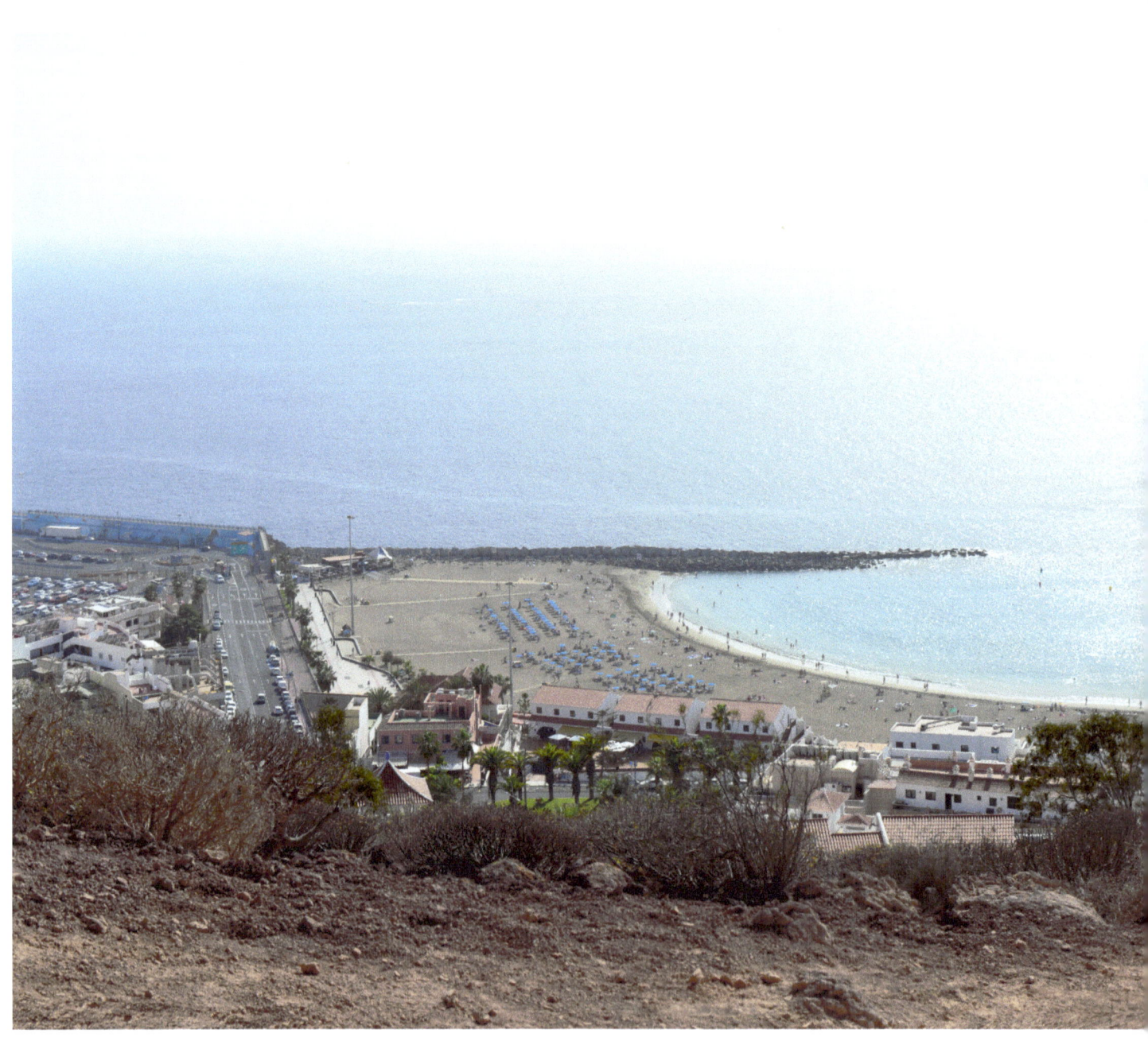

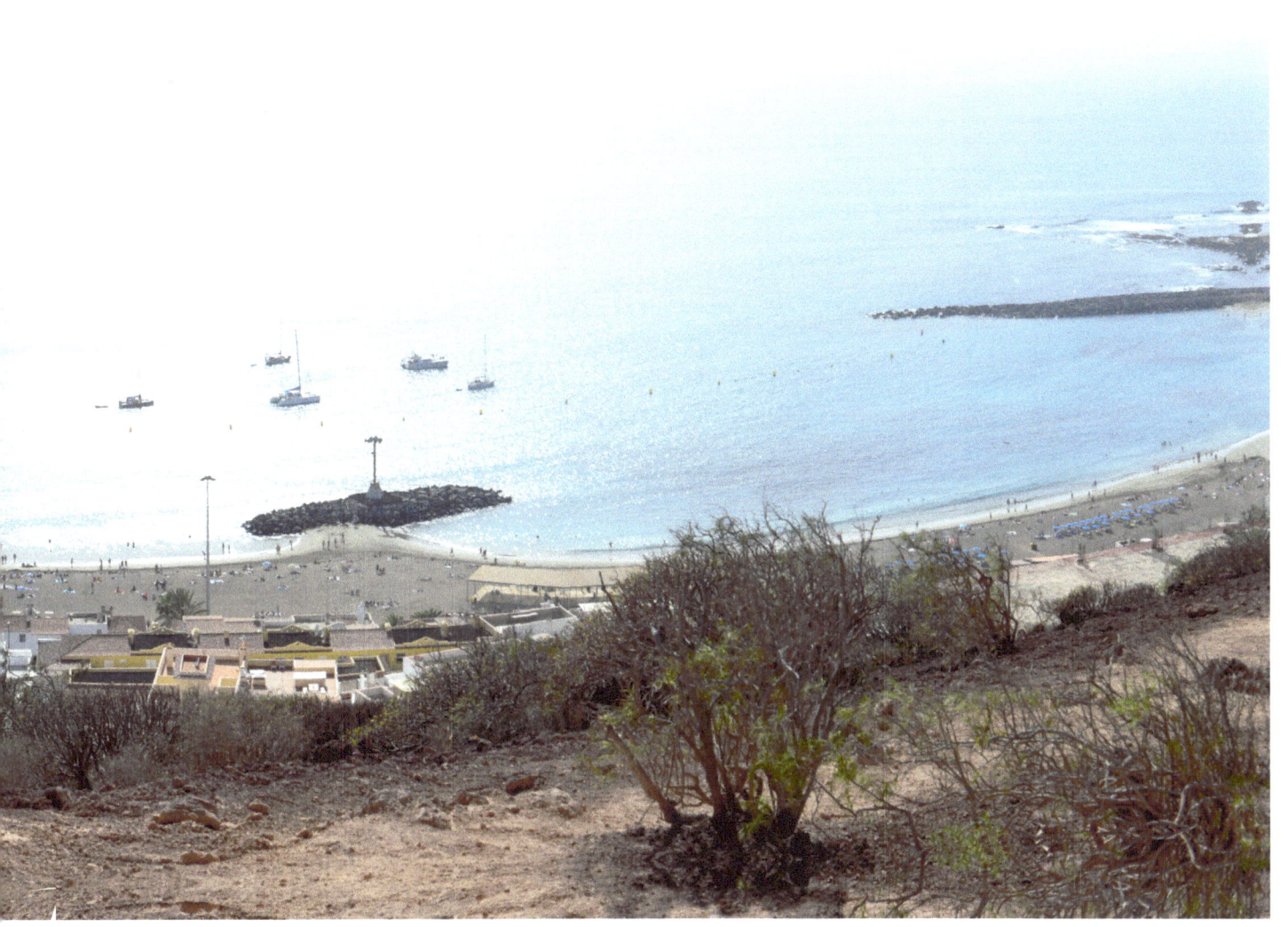

View from montana Chayofita on skyline Playa las Américas.

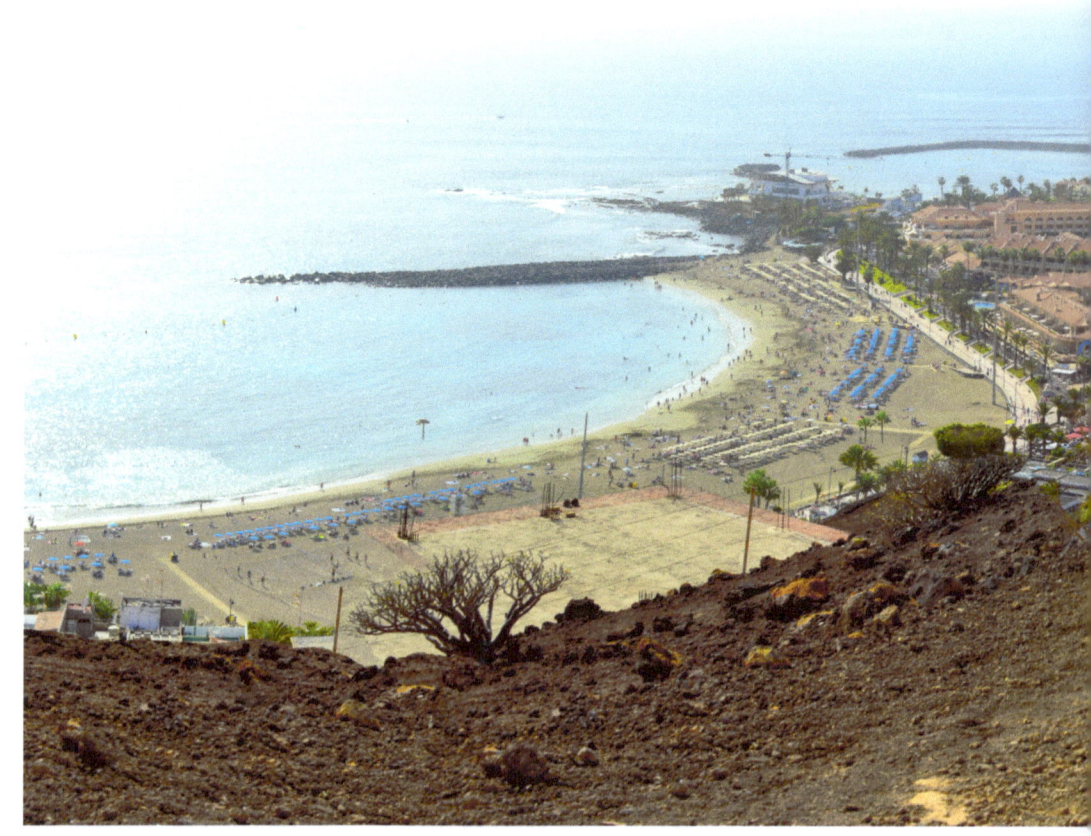

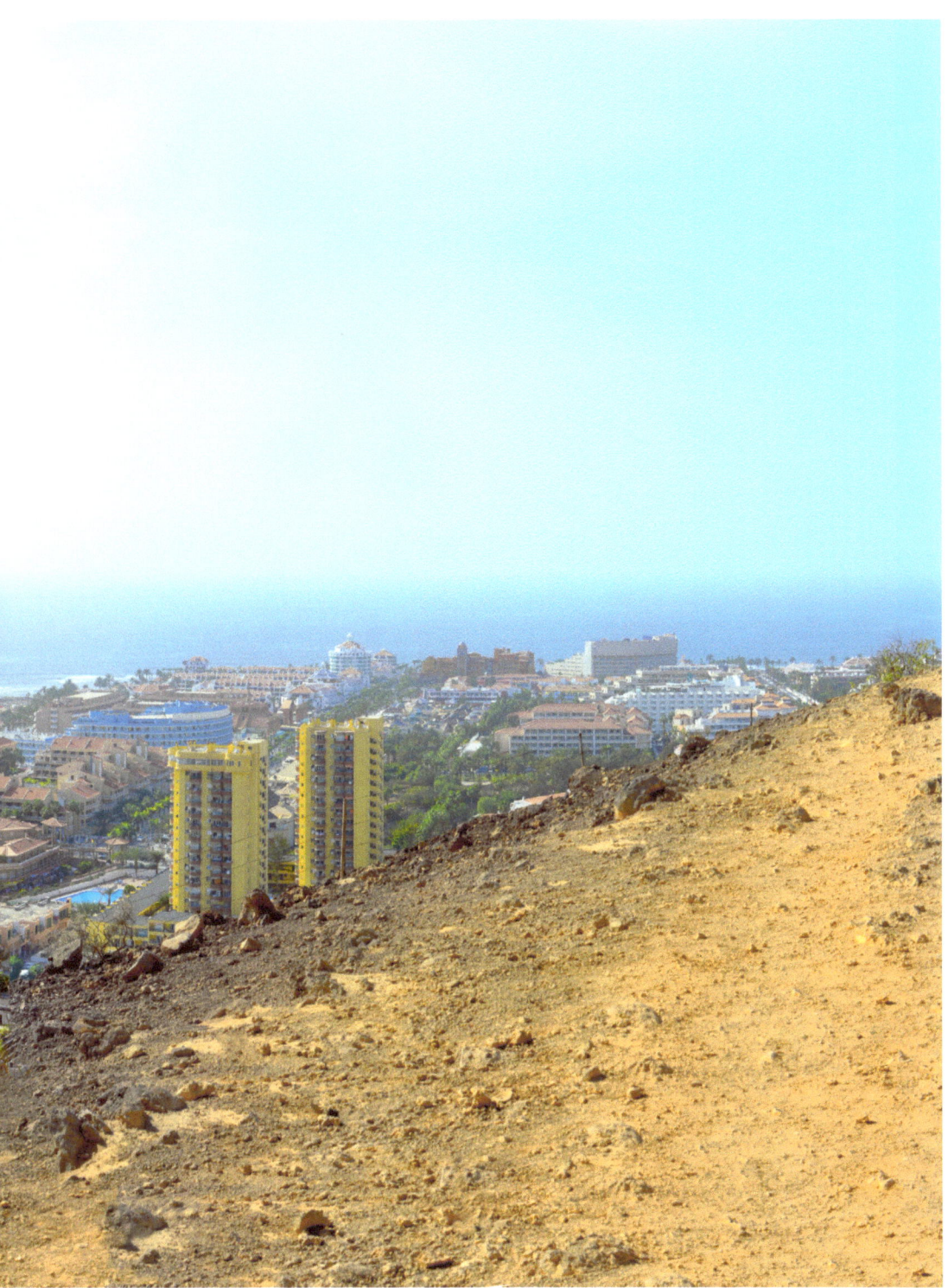

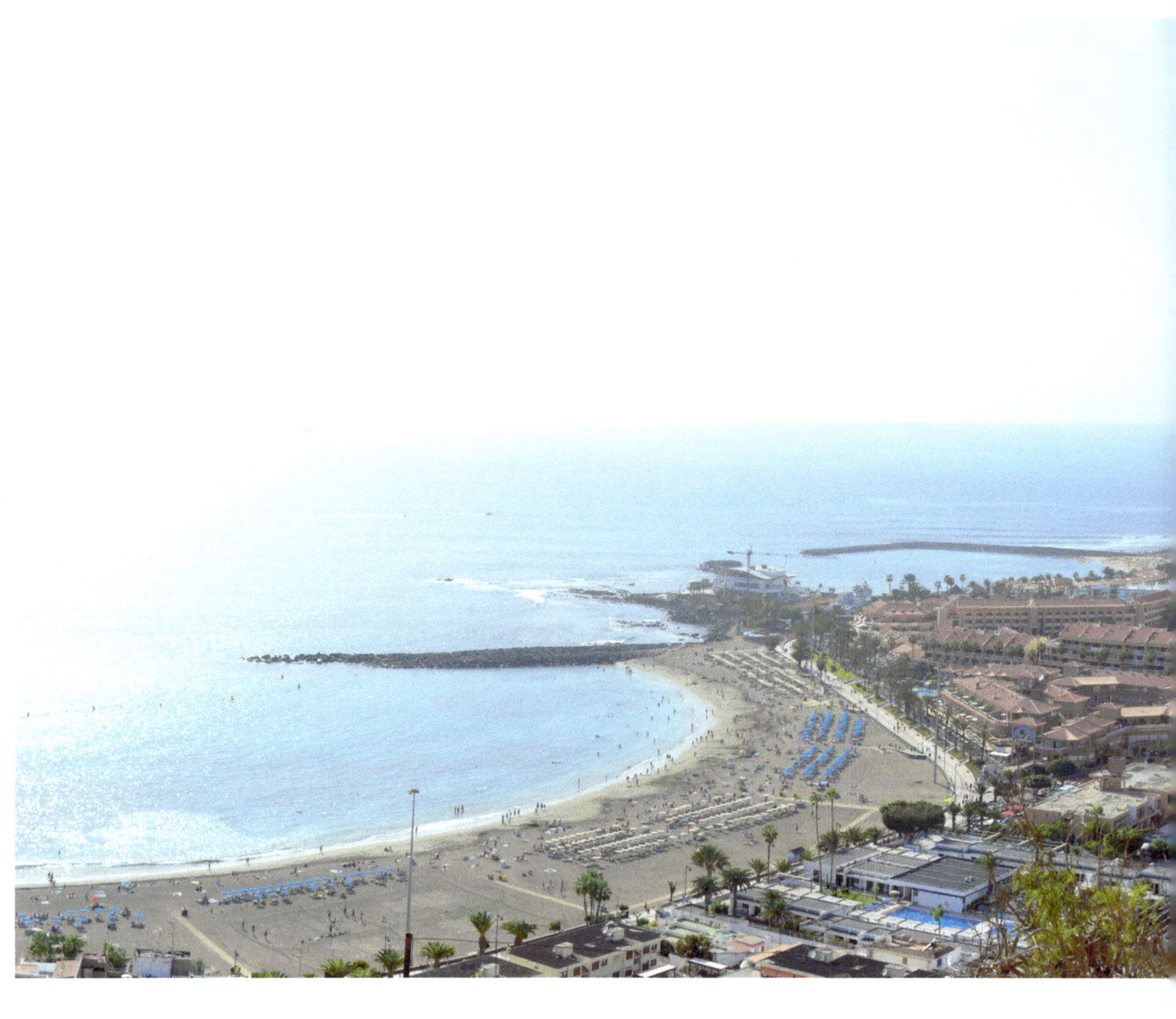

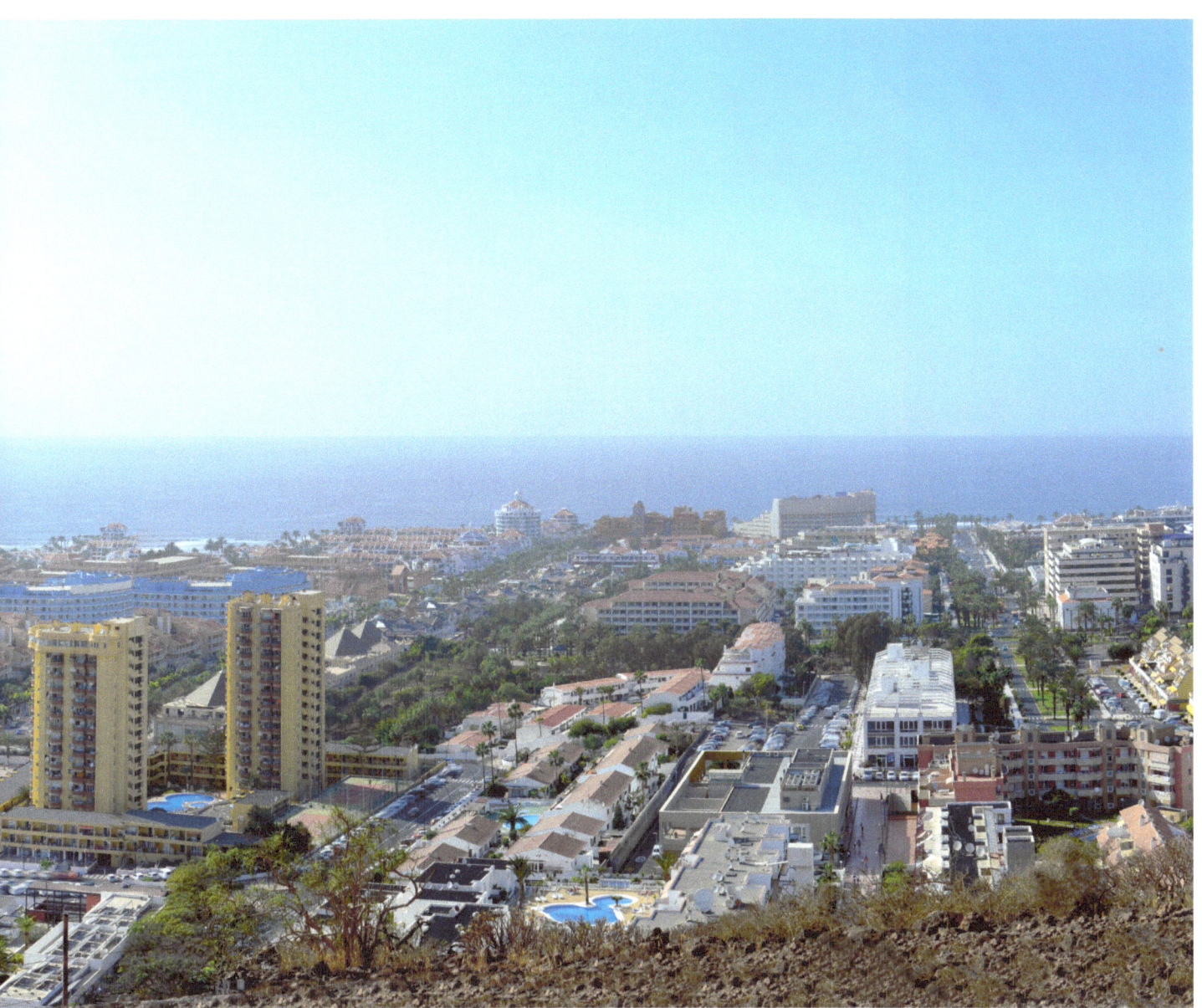

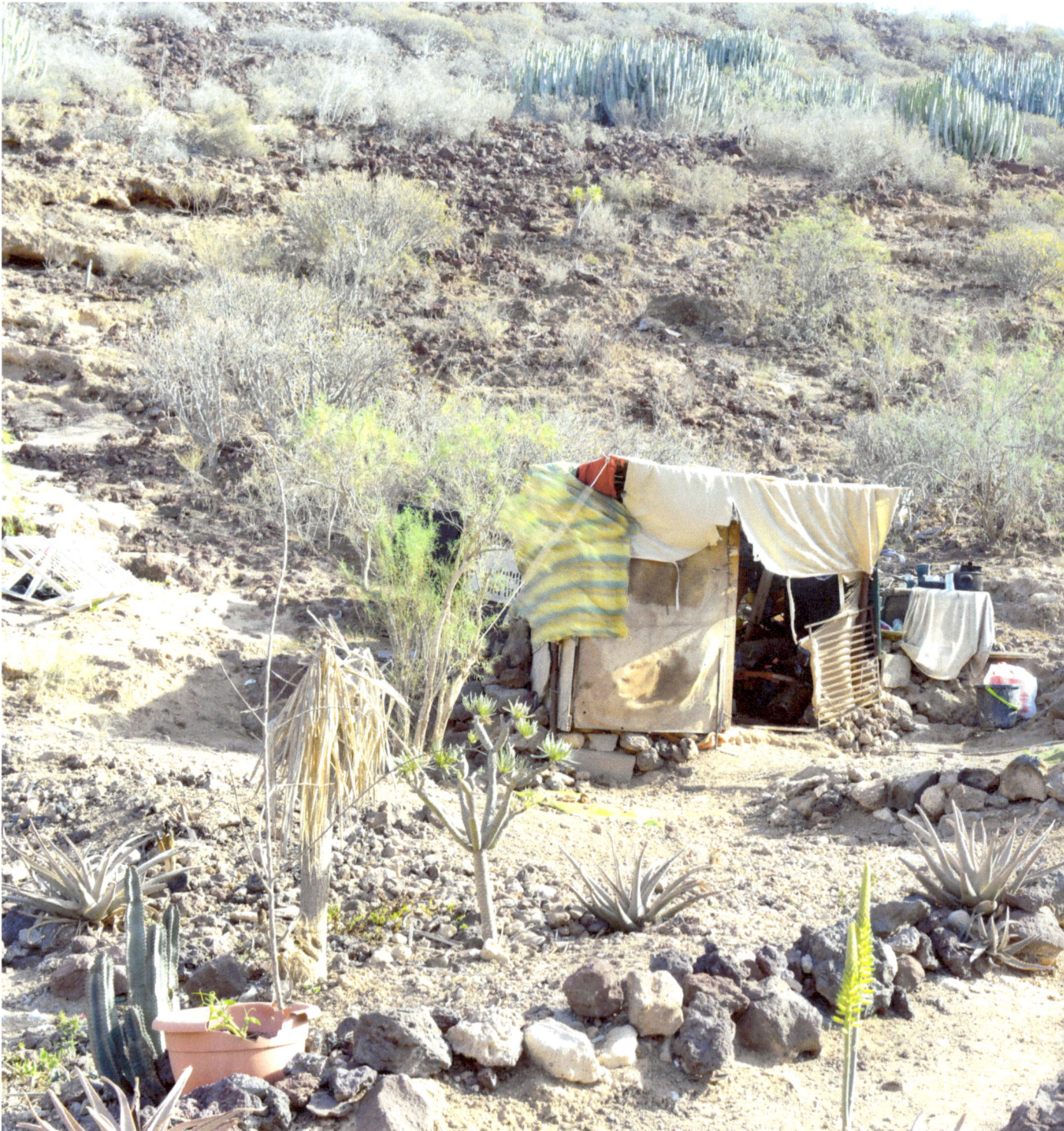

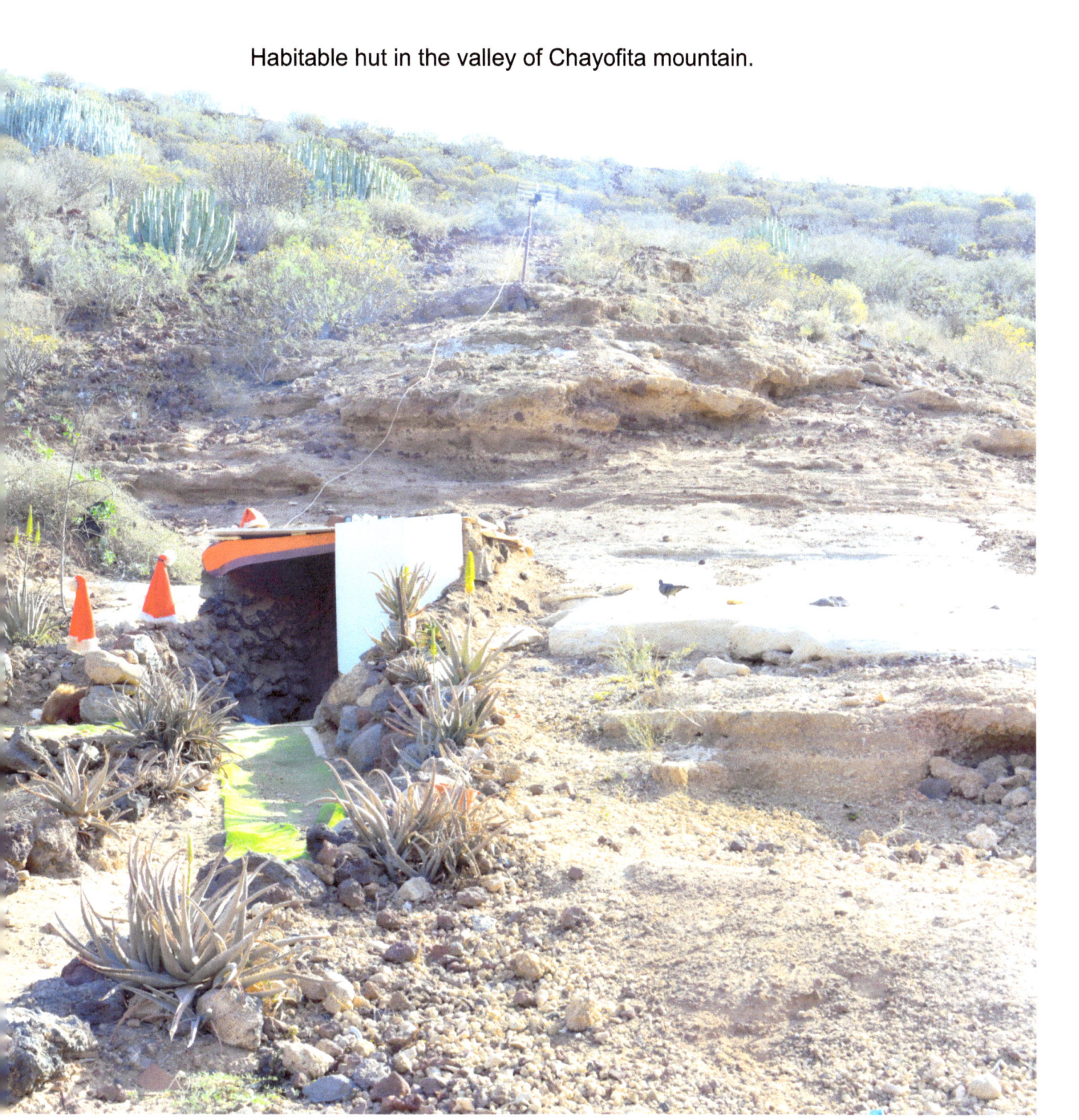
Habitable hut in the valley of Chayofita mountain.

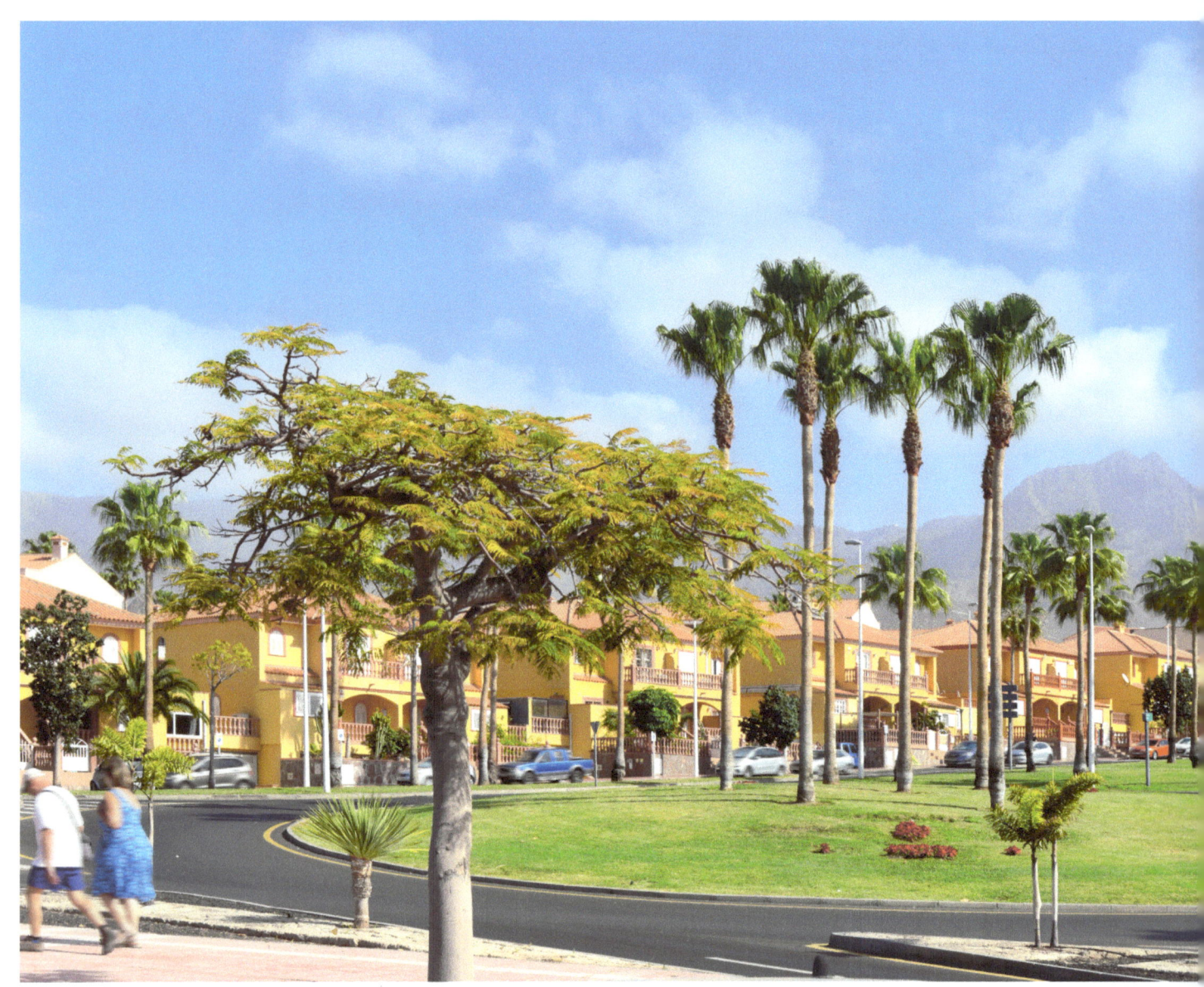

Avenida de Bruselas, Adeje.

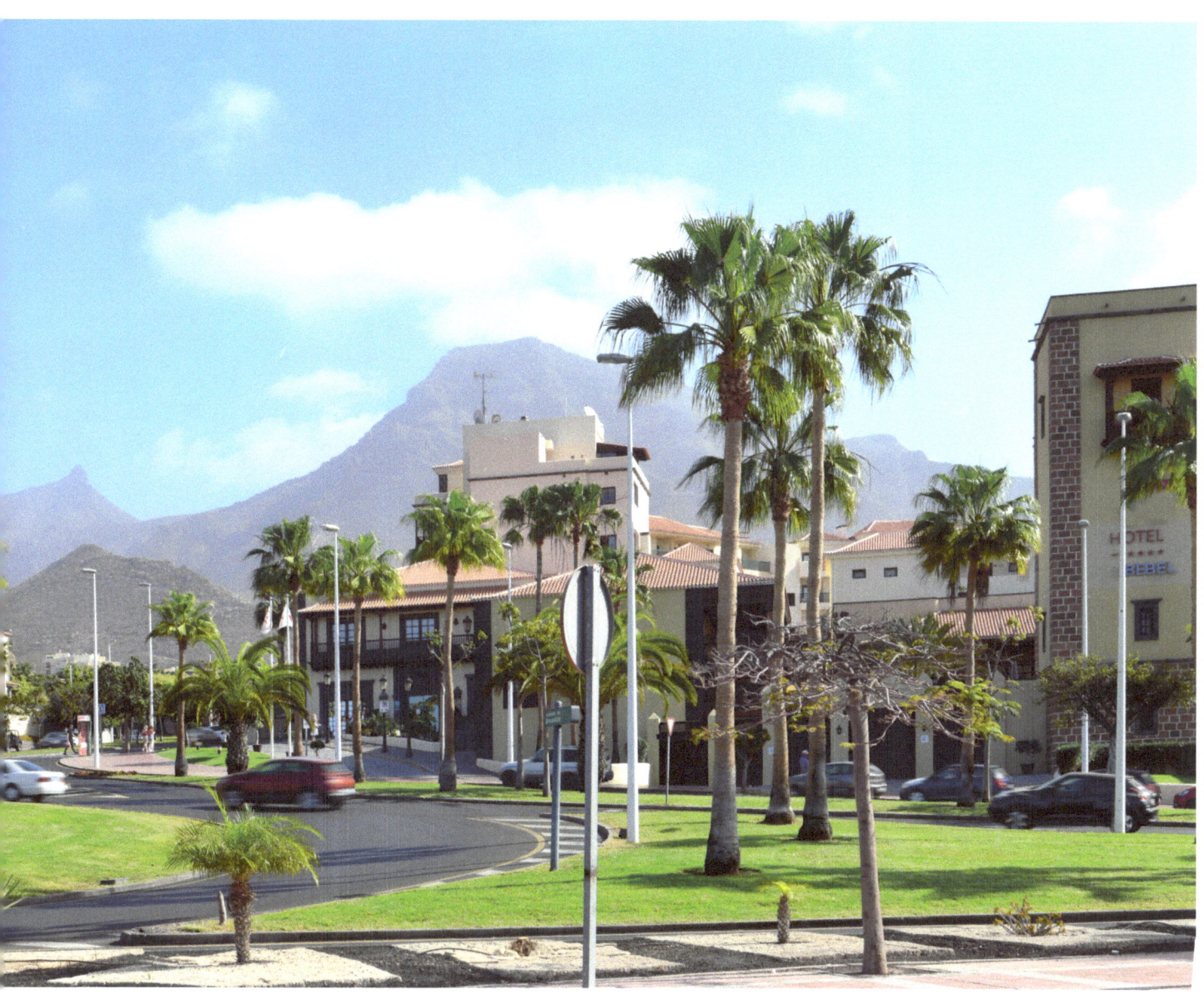

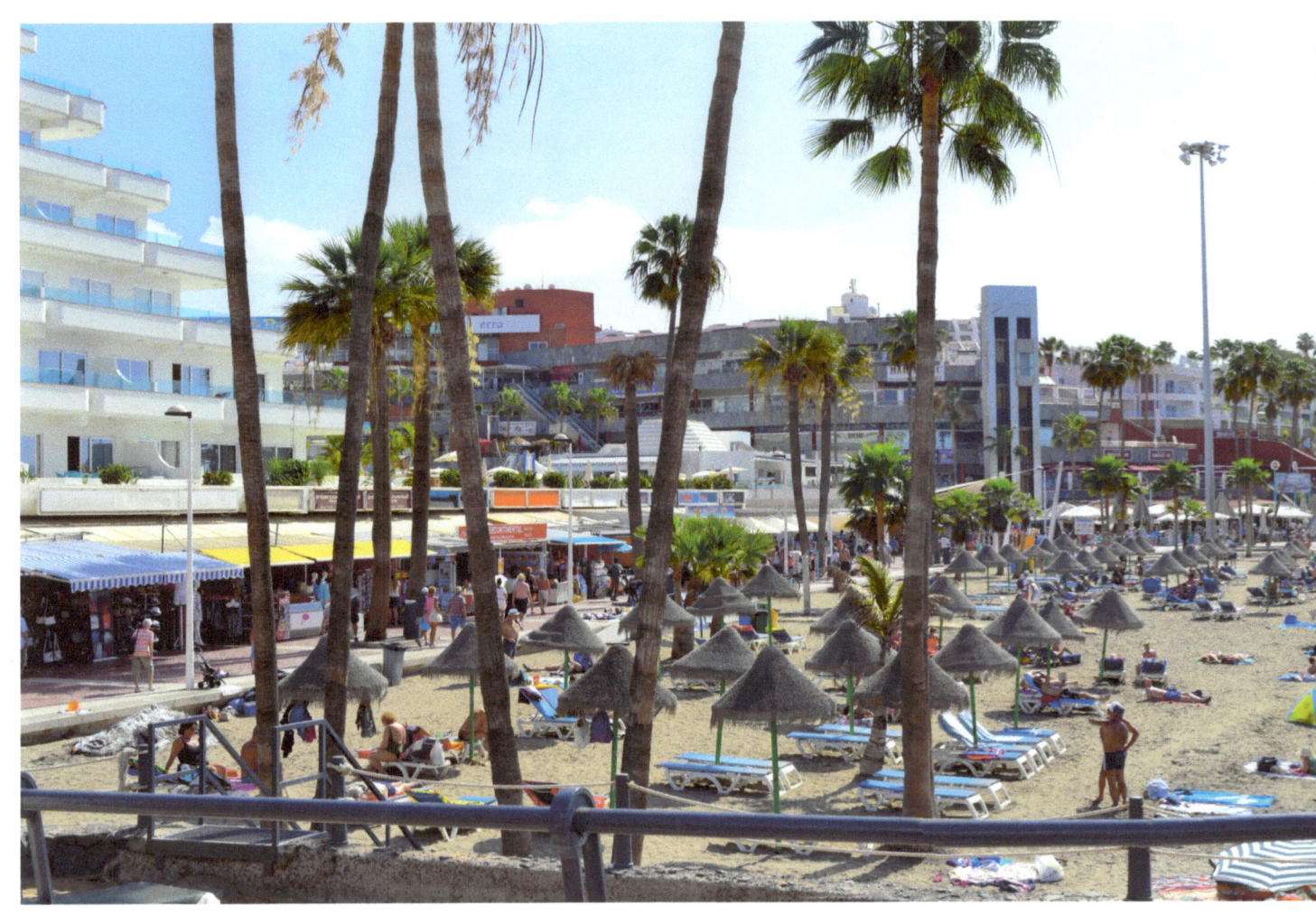

Adeje beach

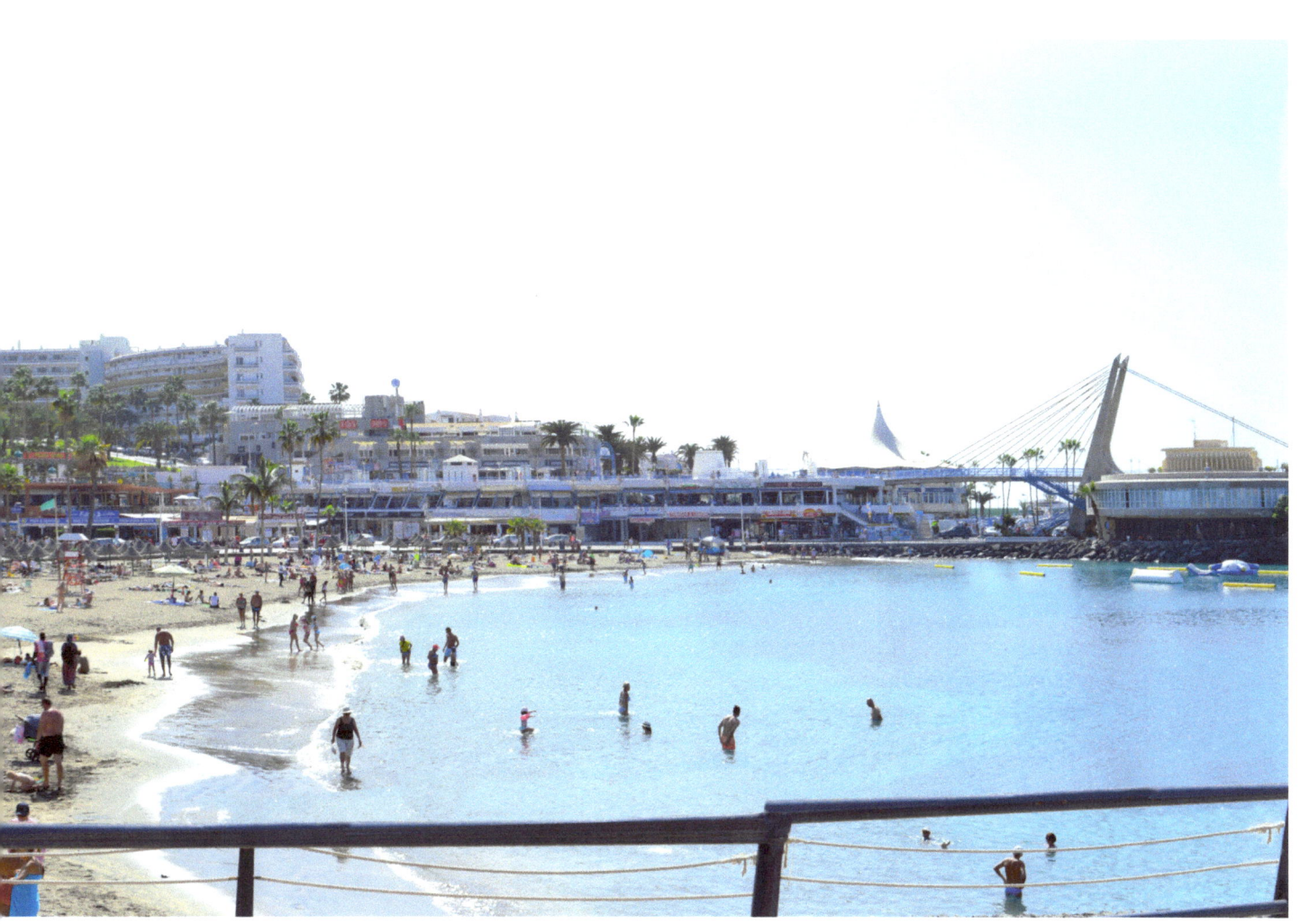

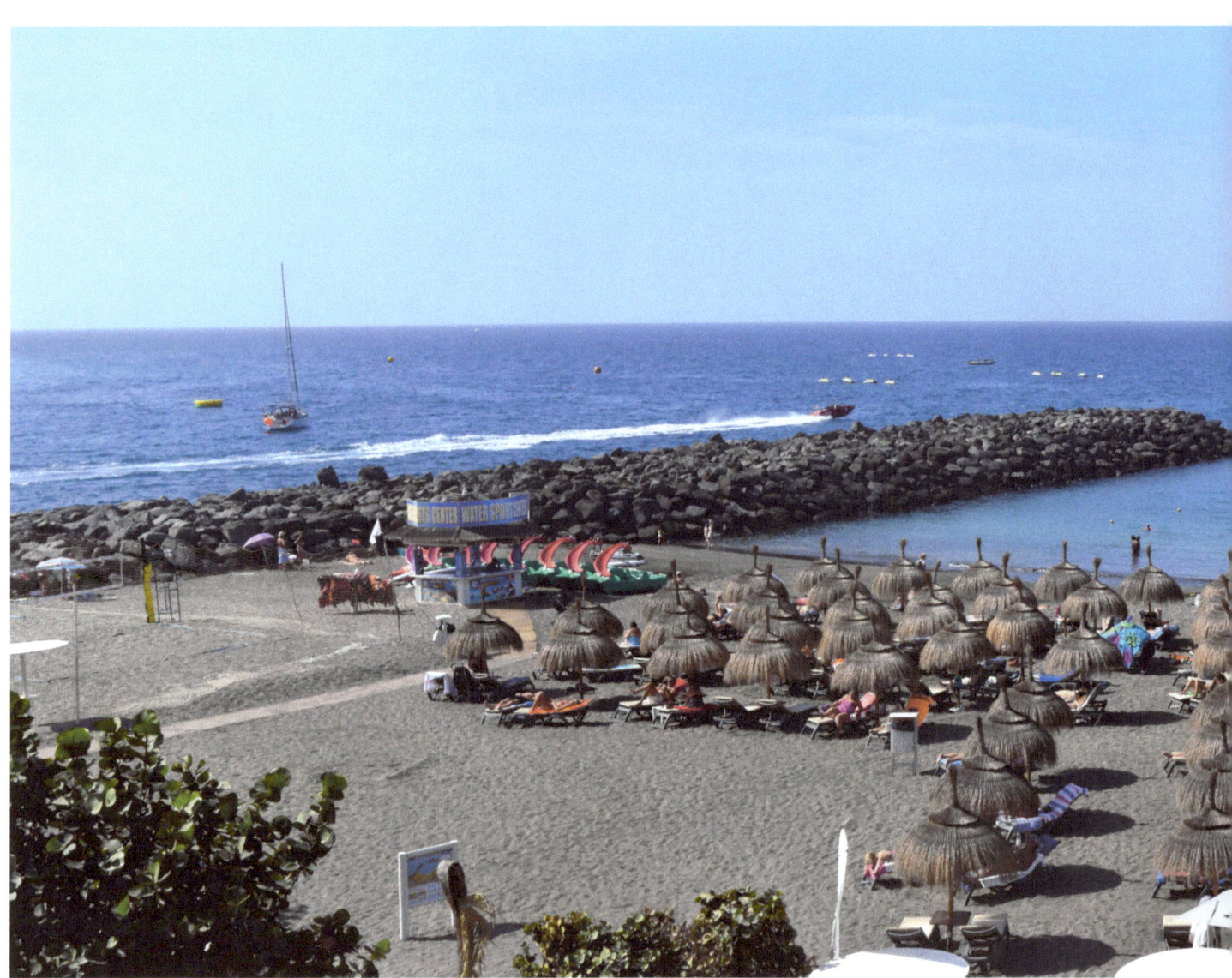

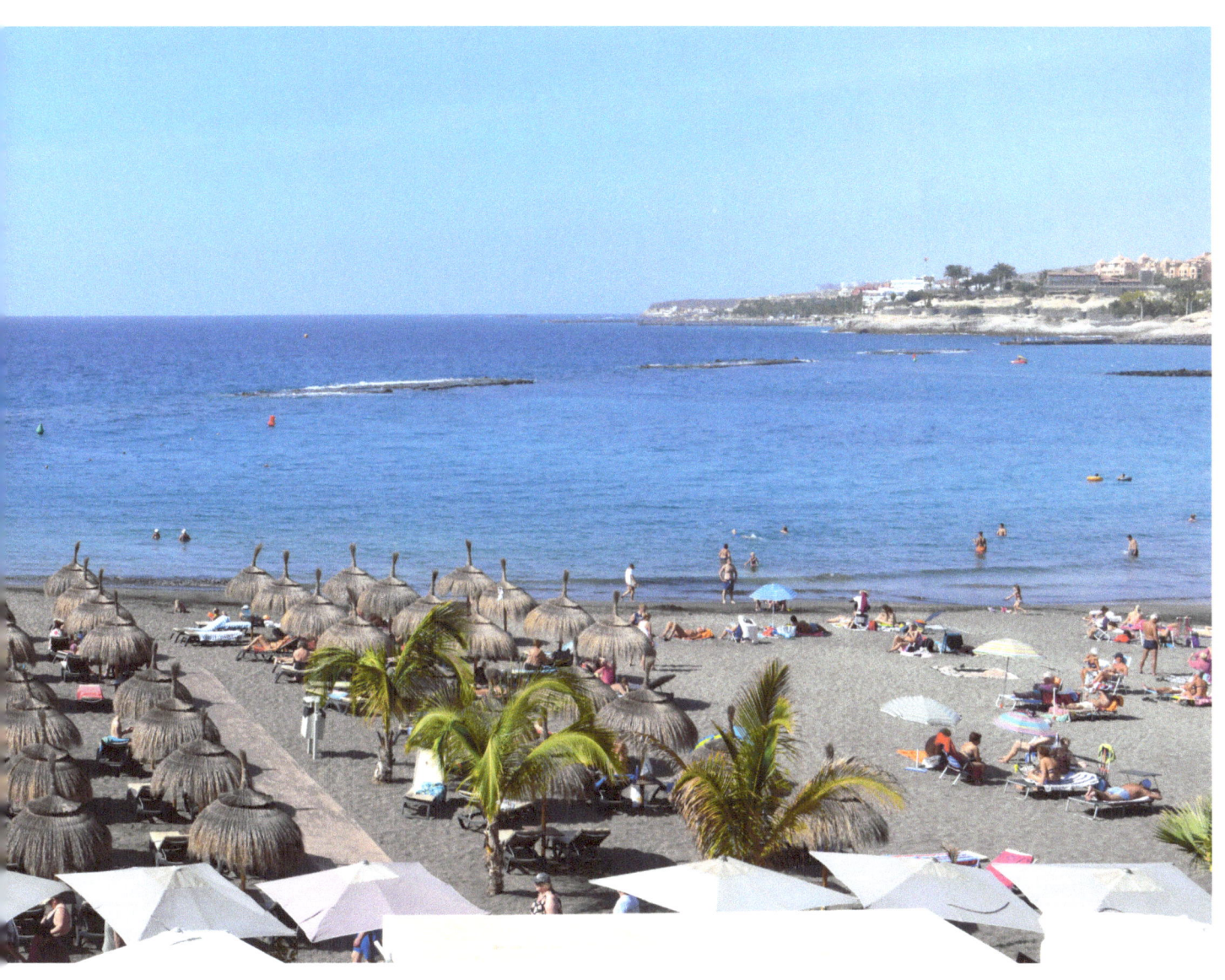

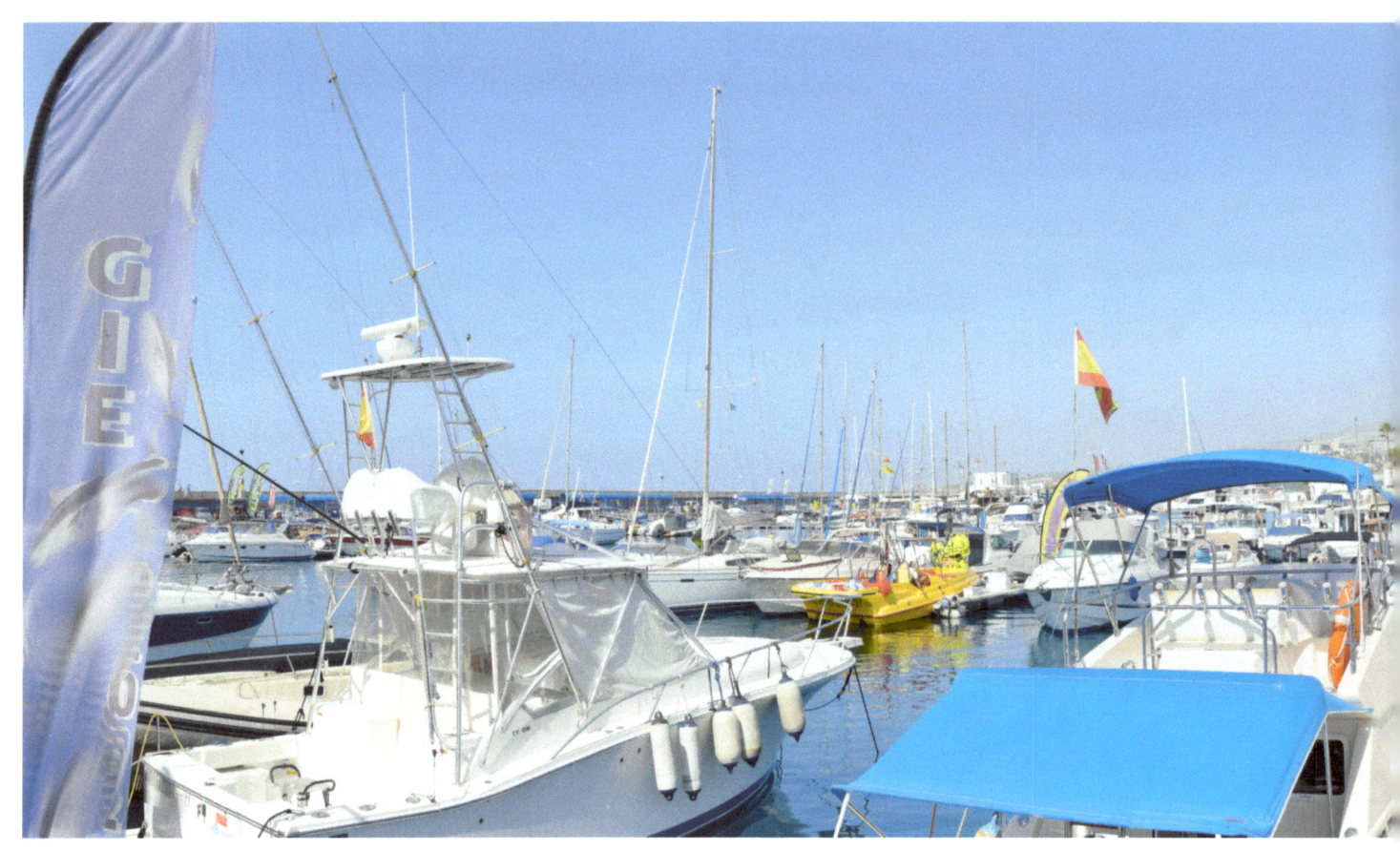

Puerto Colon marina and harbour, Costa Adeje, Playa las Américas, Tenerife Canary Islands, Spain.

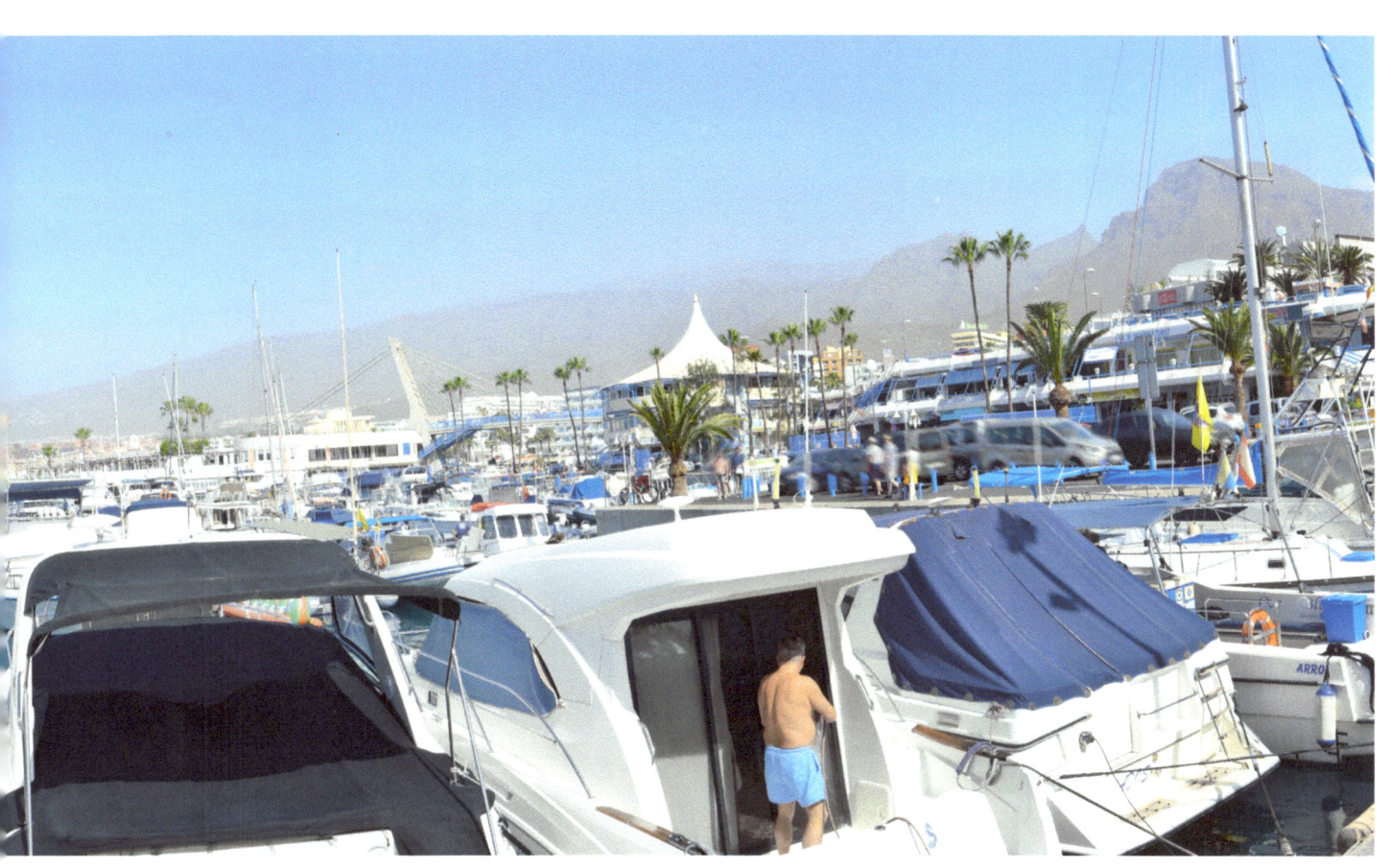

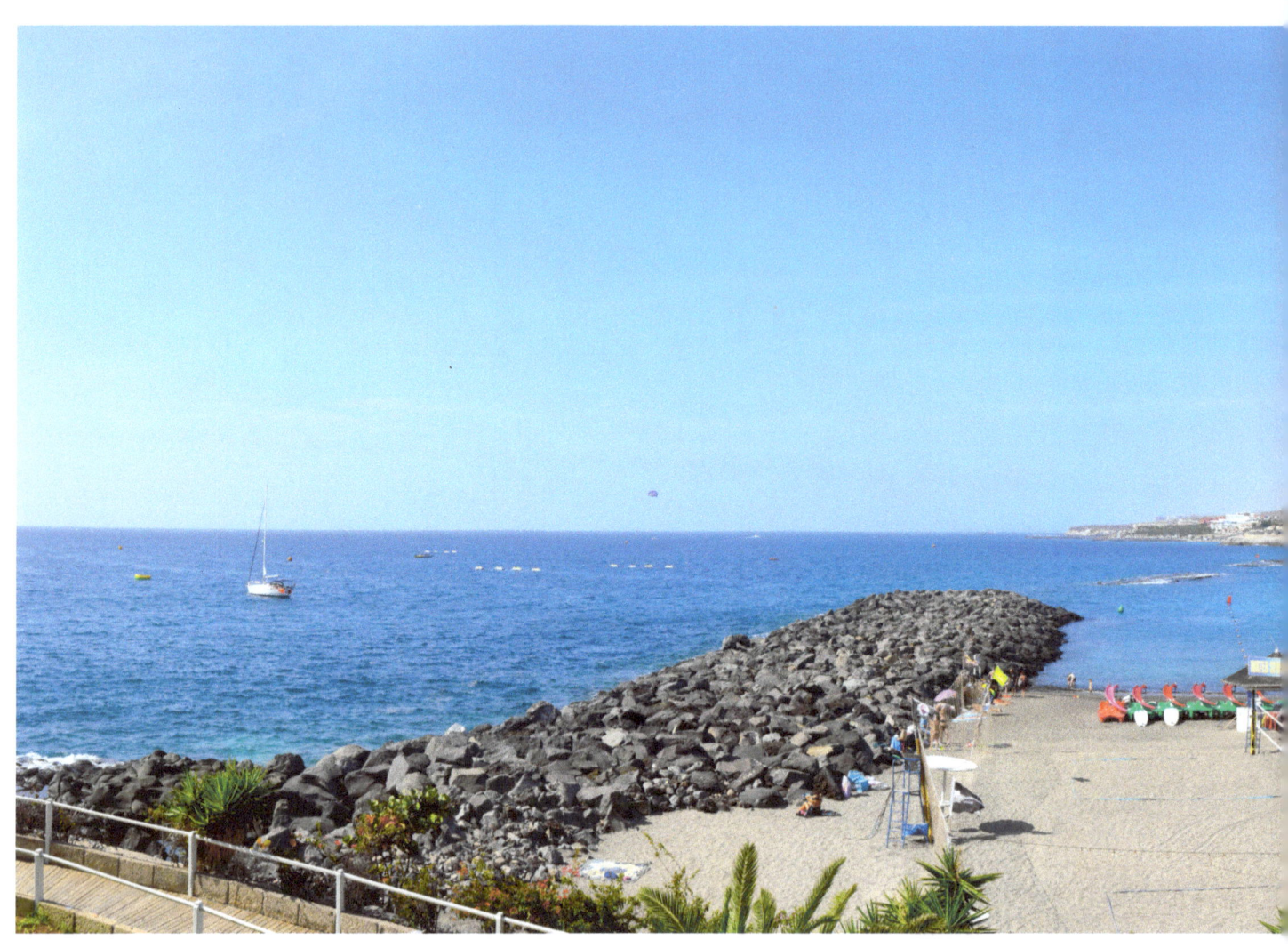

Costa Adeje beach

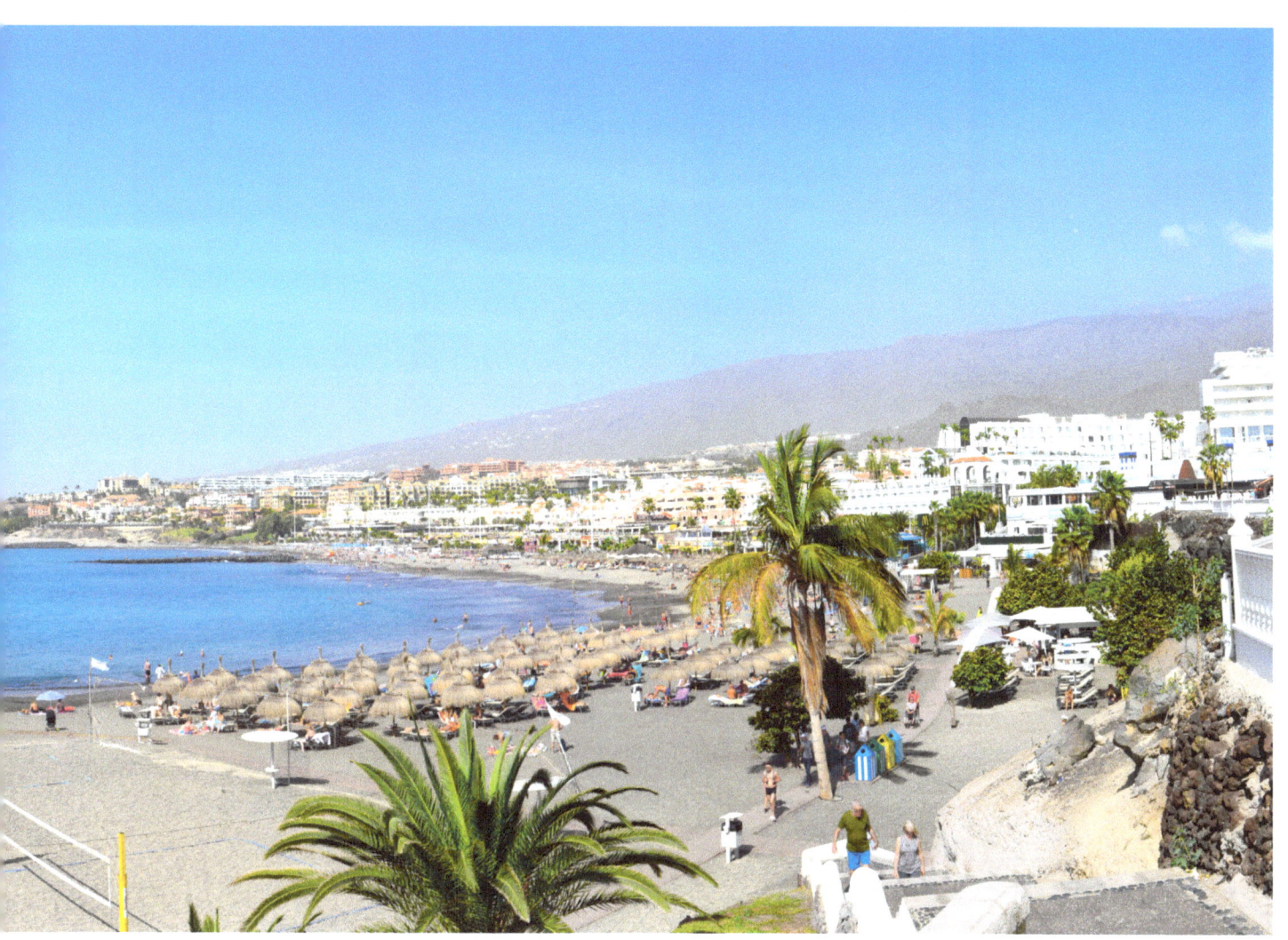

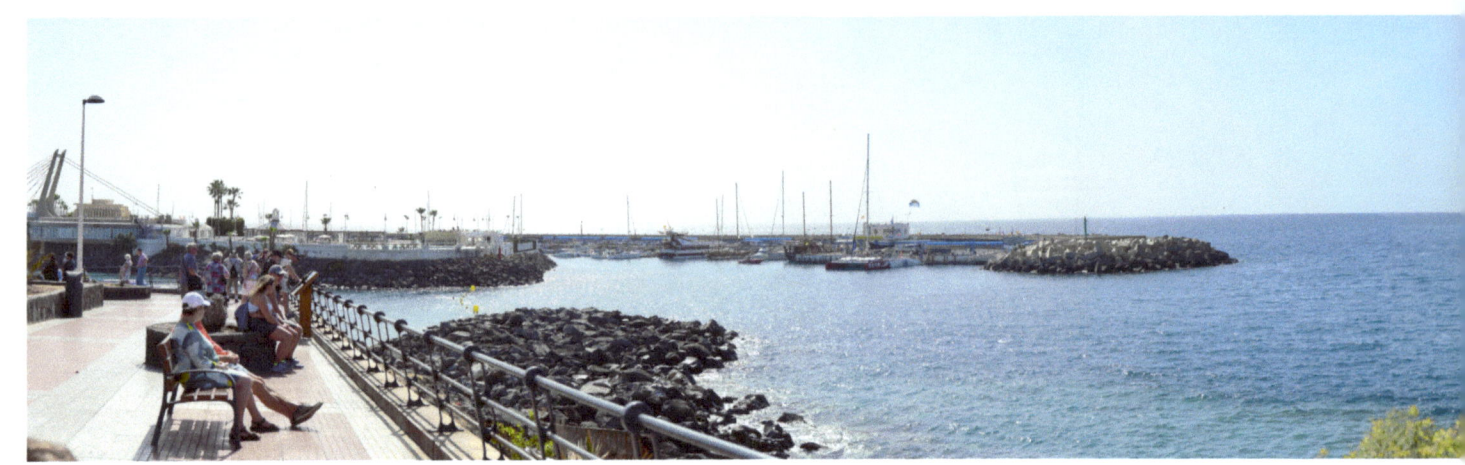

Adeje Marina.

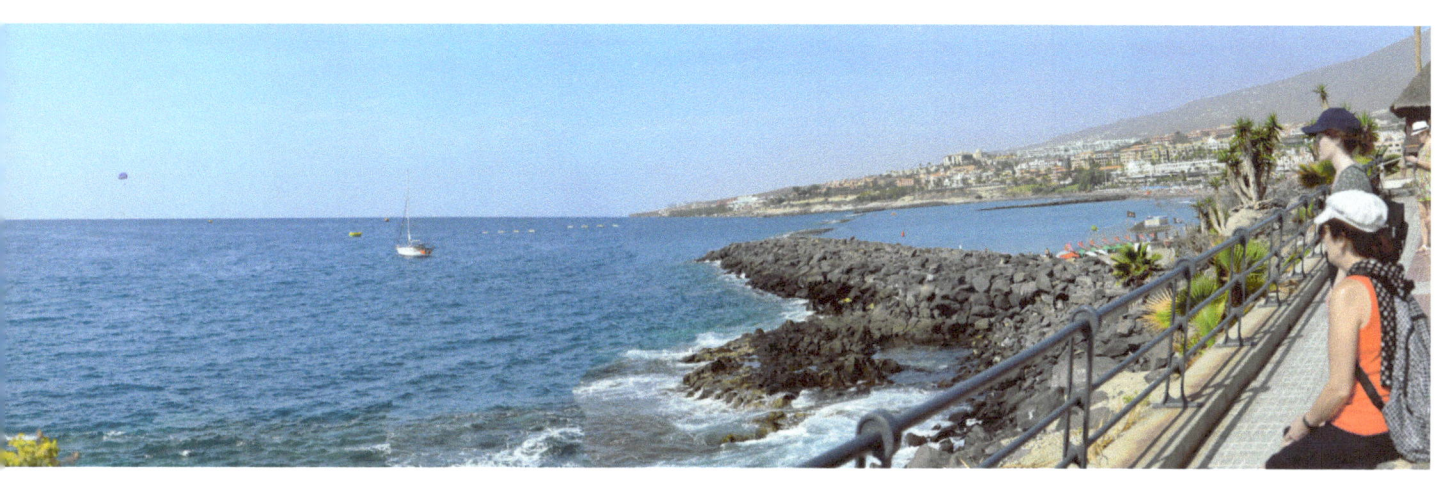

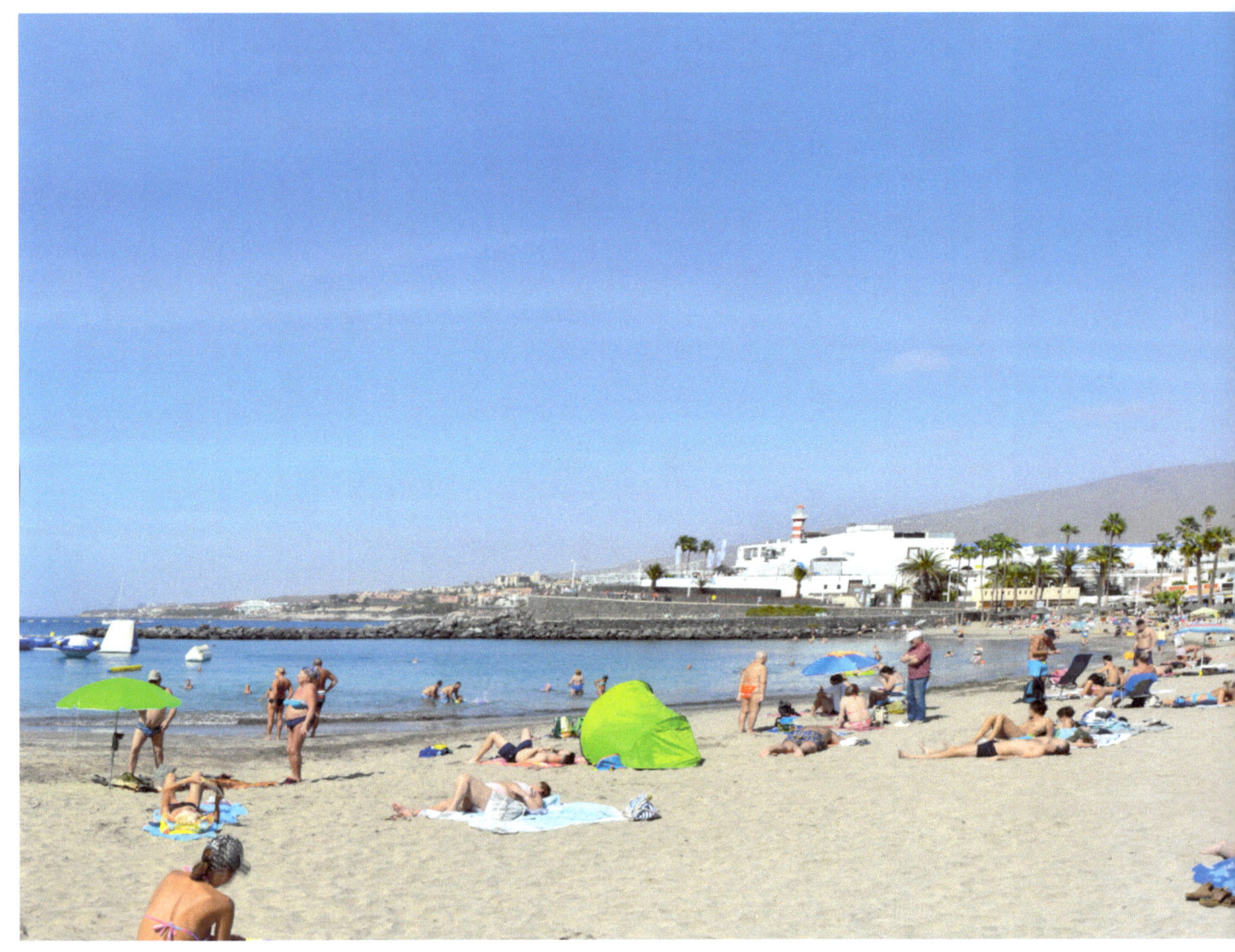

Adeje beach.

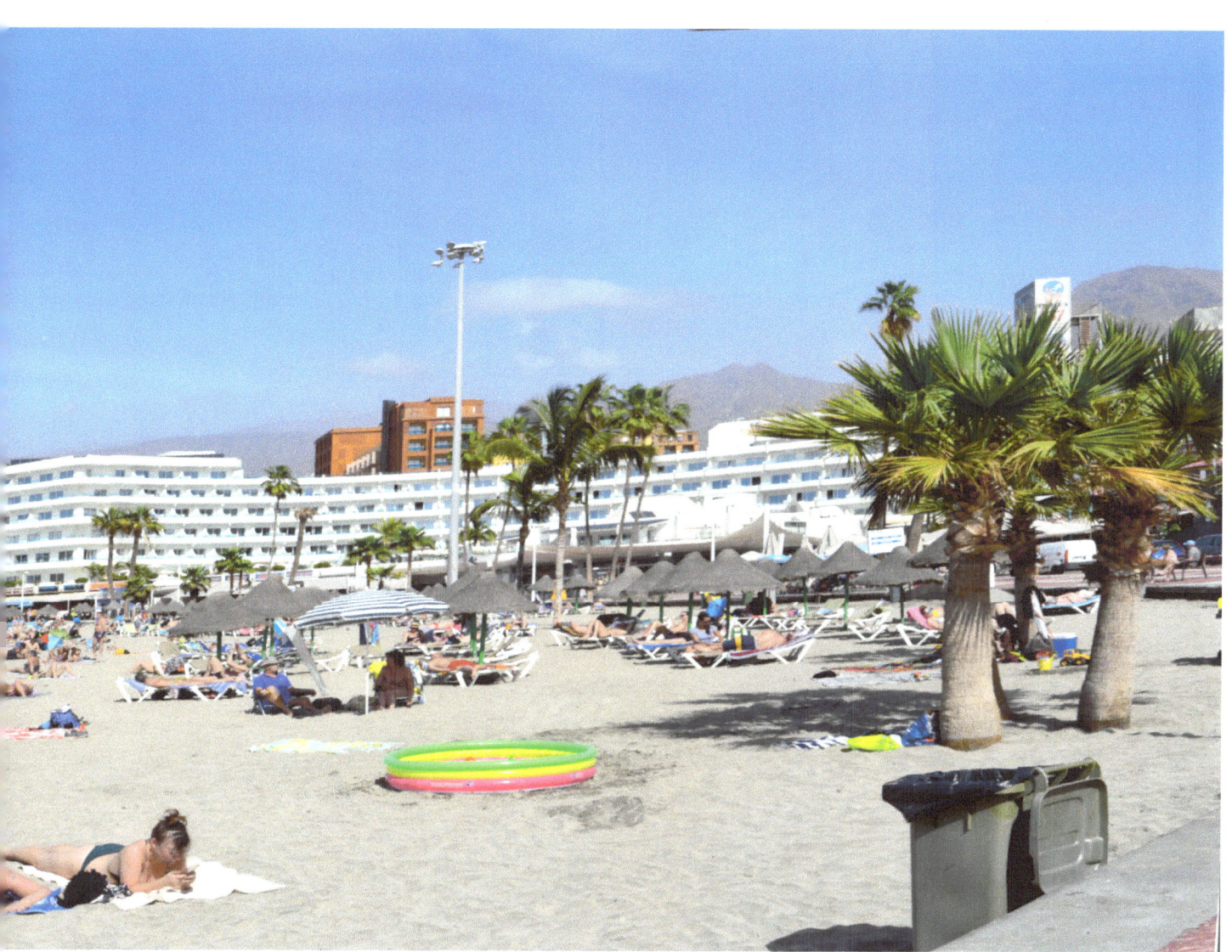

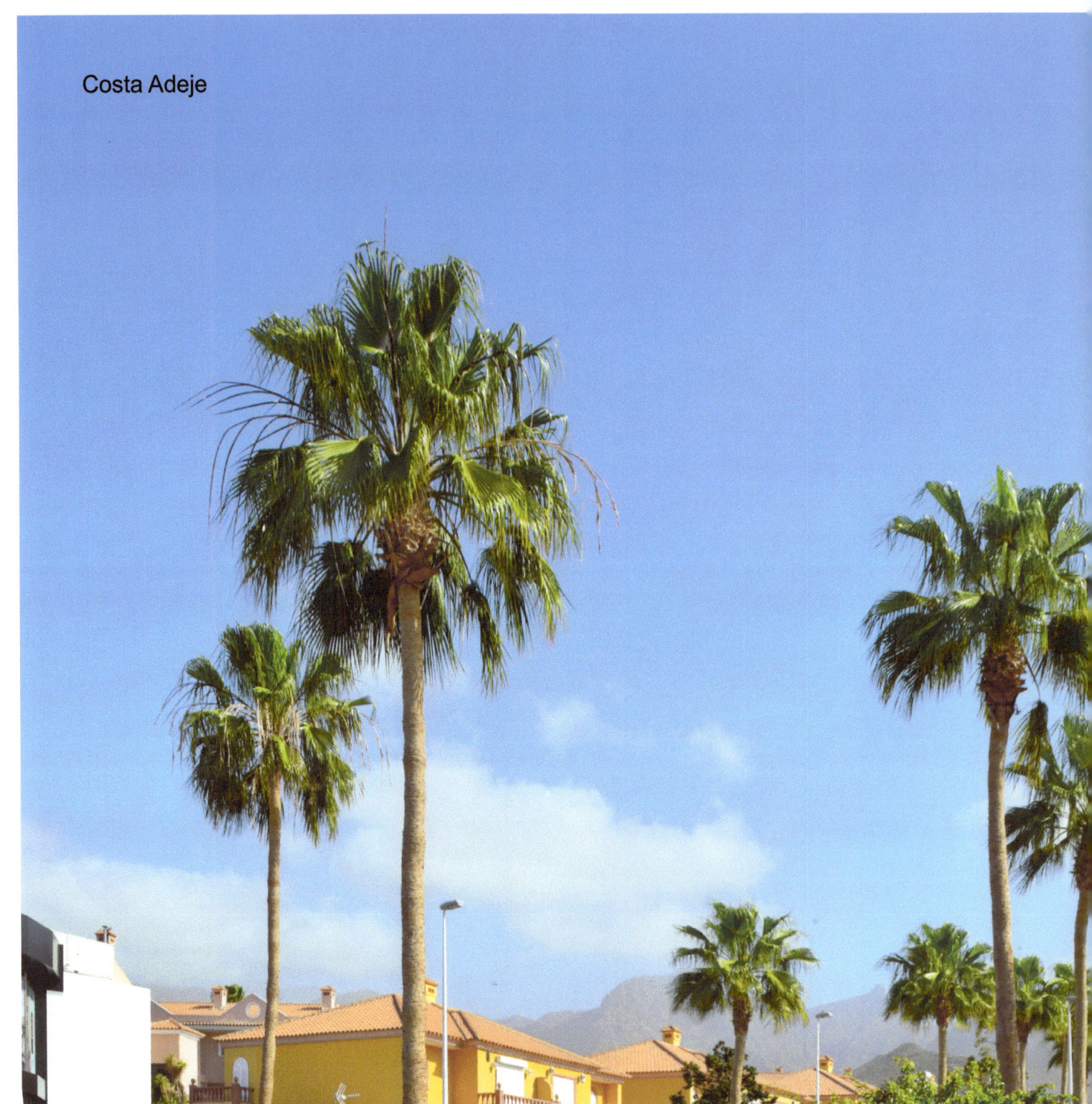
Costa Adeje

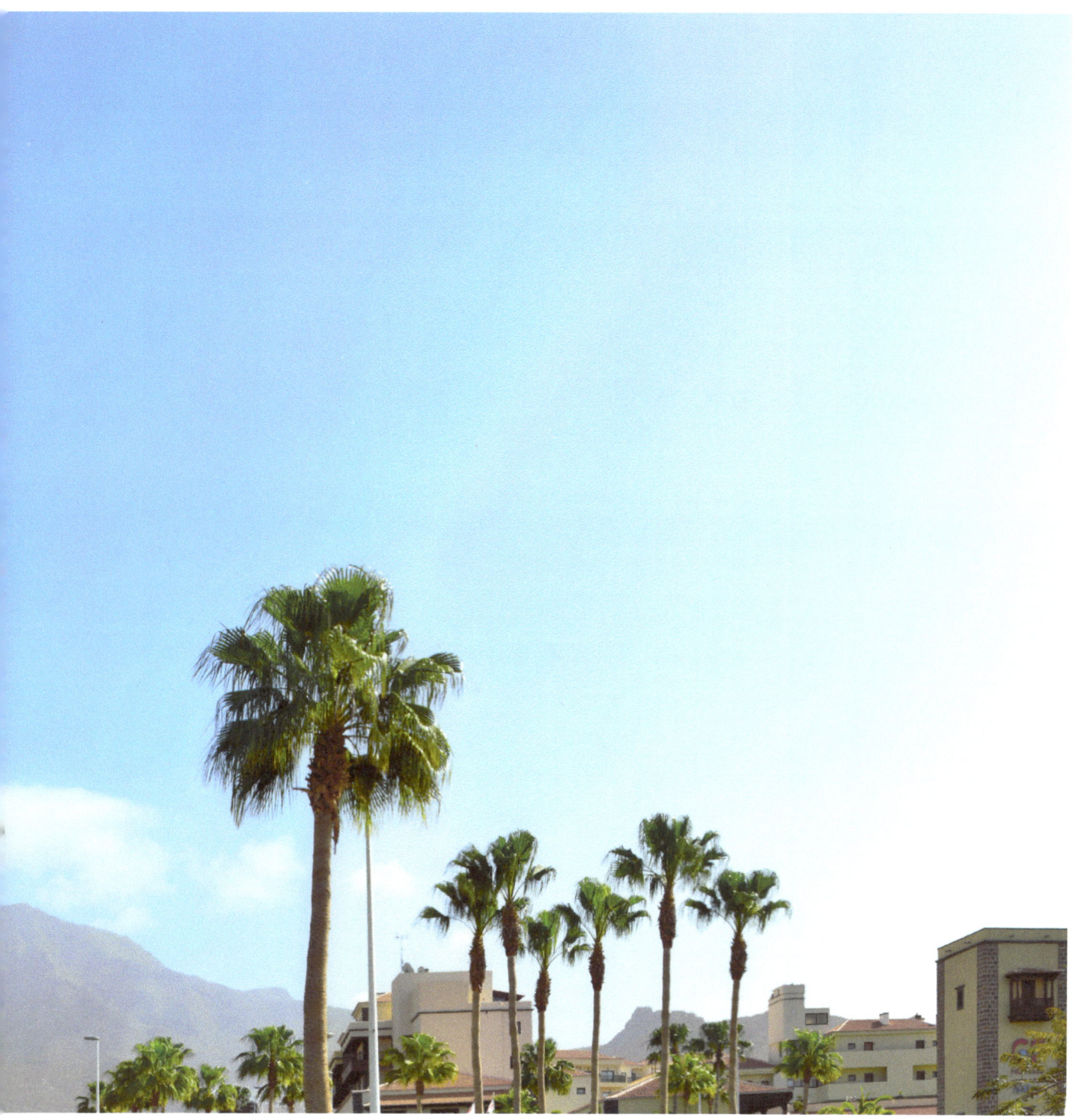

www.ingramcontent.com/pod-product-compliance
Lightning Source LLC
Chambersburg PA
CBHW051213220526
45473CB00003B/1015